'When Jesus touches some[...] continues lifelong. The we[...] the story of contemporary mission amongst an unreached people group is compelling reading. It's honest about the ordinariness and extra-ordinariness of a missionary's life; about the personal blessings and also the battles; about the 'successes' and the struggles of building and being a mission hospital in the under-resourced developing world; and at the same time it has profound lessons for faith-sharing which are as applicable in an increasingly secular Western world as in an Islamic culture. Having had the privilege of overseeing Kerry's call and commissioning it's a joy to read now of her legacy. As Kerry says "Let's not keep Jesus to ourselves, let's give him away"; if each of us rises to that challenge in the unique way for which we are created the story of the transformation of this community could become the story of the transformation in our own communities too.'

Revd John Coles, Chair, New Wine Trust, and Kerry Stillman's sending vicar from St Barnabas, North London

'Kerry captures the heart of this mission hospital whilst detailing the history and people that have shaped this special place. A gripping read that reminds us that hope can flourish even in the most arid conditions.'

Abi Estelle, consultant oral and maxillofacial surgeon, and founder of 'Willing and Abel' www.willingandabel.org.uk

'Kerry Stillman's account of her experiences while serving in mission in the north of Cameroon is beautifully written and conveys to the reader an honest, accurate and inspiring story of cross-cultural missionary service in the contemporary world. The context in which she worked can truly be described as "off the beaten track", both in terms of the remoteness of this area of West Africa, and with regard to the Muslim people who live there. The narrative of the establishing of a Christian hospital in that situation, of the devoted service of its founders and staff, and of their loving service of a community afflicted by poverty, disease and, more recently, terrorism, is profoundly moving and challenging. Kerry's own story is interwoven with that of the hospital and is full of fascinating experiences, shared with passion, honesty and love.'

Dr David W. Smith, Honorary Lecturer,
Centre for Ministry Studies, University of Aberdeen

'Wow. An amazing story of God's faithfulness and how he brought committed and gifted believers from around the world to serve, care for, and reach out to an isolated Muslim tribal community in northern Cameroon. This is no documentary. It's an exciting story full of desperate pleas, answered prayers, miraculous healings, thwarted terrorists, even love and romance! A real live adventure of the worldwide body of Christ pulling together against incredible odds to meet the physical and spiritual needs of these unreached people. In heaven someday, you'll meet some of them! Until then, here is their story . . .'

Dr Steve Shadrach, Global Ambassador,
Center for Mission Mobilization www.mobilization.org

'I remember vividly my first trip to this hospital in Cameroon over a decade ago. My heart was deeply touched by the physical and spiritual needs of the people in the region, as well as by the love and compassion of those ministering through the hospital. In her book *Blood, Sweat and Jesus*, Kerry Stillman opens a door for us to experience God's life-changing work in a part of the world most people rarely think about. Your heart will be touched as you read the stories of the message of the gospel lived out through the love of God's people in a small Christian hospital in the midst of Muslims.'

Kevin Kompelien, President,
Evangelical Free Church of America

'Kerry Stillman has written a vivid account of establishing a flagship Christian hospital in Muslim-dominated Northern Cameroon, with all the highs and the lows, the grime and the glory. Through this remarkable story she has managed to simultaneously both debunk the romance of missions and relay an inspiring account of God's adventurers doing extraordinary things in sub-Saharan Africa. But her main focus is on the local Muslim people. Full of real-life stories, this is a moving chronicle of God at work that touched my heart and transported me back to the time when I had the privilege of visiting Kerry and her friends in the dusty lanes of that village.'

Revd Henry Kendal, Vicar of St Barnabas,
North London, UK

'Pioneers UK has been gladly sending missionaries to this hospital in Cameroon for a quarter of a century. Kerry, herself, first went there in 1998. It is my complete privilege to warmly commend Kerry's own story; wrapped up in the story of this remarkable hospital and in the lives of so many who both ministered and were ministered to in this place. In the centre of Kerry's engaging and challenging history is a line which, for me, sums up the heart of her book: "However, right in the middle of it, Jesus walked in." *Blood, Sweat and Jesus* is not just the story of a hospital, but also a challenging insight into the interface between Christians and Muslims – particularly Fulbe Muslims. Kerry writes with heart and soul, discernment and experience.'

Stephen Carling, Director, Pioneers, UK

Blood, Sweat and Jesus

The story of a Christian hospital bringing hope and healing in a Muslim community

Kerry Stillman

First published 2020 by Authentic Media Limited,
PO Box 6326, Bletchley, Milton Keynes, MK1 9GG.
authenticmedia.co.uk

British Library Cataloguing in Publication Data
A catalogue record for this book is available from the British Library.
ISBN: 978-1-78893-148-9
978-1-78893-149-6 (e-book)

Most Cameroonians mentioned in this book have had
their names changed to protect their identity.

Cover design by Jennifer Burrell, Fresh Vision Design
Printed and bound by CPI Group (UK) Ltd, Croydon, CR0 4YY

Contents

Foreword

What is the hardest thing you have done?

My first trip to Cameroon, and Meskine Hospital, was in the fall of 2003. I was invited to travel as a new board member and be an encouragement to the missionaries and the employees of the hospital. Having worked in healthcare finance for most of my forty-year career, I thought I understood the invitation. It was my first time to the huge continent of Africa, but I had a couple of international trips under my belt. Truly, I did not know what I did not know!

For that trip, and the five subsequent visits to the hospital, being open to learn and willing to adapt to change helped me acclimatize to the sub-Saharan world I had never known. But best of all, making that first trip introduced me to strangers who are now my closest friends. And that first trip changed the trajectory of my career as I stepped into the stateside leadership of the Medical Centers of West Africa (MCWA) in 2008, eventually turning a volunteer board position into my full-time vocation. It was a huge shift, and I have been told that what I did was too hard to do.

Like on the field, the MCWA board in Baton Rouge has included more than fifty people who agreed to work together for the same purpose: to see Christ's kingdom extended among those still in darkness. What a privilege to serve together with highly qualified bankers and physicians, engineers and teachers, home-makers and attorneys, accountants and human resource trainers, and so many more categories of talent. The diversity of our backgrounds and life experiences blended as only God could design, so we could be one voice before God and before MCWA supporters and friends. I have been challenged, encouraged and stretched by these fellow board members, and I could not serve in my role without the unconditional loving kindness given me by these volunteers. Like unseen stagehands in a theatre production, the show would simply not go on without them.

I want you to know the people of this story. Kerry has told a most personal story and I am excited for her words and her heart to be before you. Writing a biography is a vulnerable act. She has not held back in writing of the harder things she experienced in her life in Cameroon. She has been honourable and humorous in her style of revealing episodes of her life as a physiotherapist who wants to talk of Jesus wherever she goes. Her grace, poise and gentleness are revealed along with her passion, boldness and fun-loving energy.

If you think, 'I could never do that!' then this book is for you. The secret is that none of these friends thought they could do what was asked of them at some point in their time in the far north province. Impossible – and yet this story of twenty-five years of a medical mission hospital is before you. Meskine Hospital offered compassionate healthcare to all who came, with the desire to make Jesus known, and the story unfolded in the improbable steps of men, women and children from every walk of life who came together in a way bigger than any one of them could have planned or imagined.

I do want you to find adventure in the life of a young woman – a woman who is quite special to me. Read this book to consider what you learn about yourself when you read the hard episodes of death, torment, anguish and unanswered questions. Heartaches, systemic social brokenness and unrelenting need in West Africa will build tension and heaviness in your heart. But most of all, I want you to read this book and look for Jesus. He is present in this story; do you see him? I pray that you will see that the greatest needs are met by the greatest love of my Saviour and Lord.

Cheryl Yennie
Executive Director, Medical Centers of West Africa (USA)

Acknowledgements

I have endeavoured to make this book about Meskine Hospital and the people who passed through it as much as possible, rather than my personal memoir. Inevitably my story and experiences are threaded through it, but I hope it is much more than that. In order to give a fuller, more faithful account of what God has done through Meskine Hospital it has been essential to raid the memory bank of many others. This book would not have been possible without these wonderful people who offered their treasured memories for this book. My special thanks primarily goes to Scott and Lee Pyles who contributed so much, dug deep and pulled out the gems. They put up with my constant stream of questions and have been my immediate 'go to' sound board for everything. Essentially, this is their book, as they have been an 'on field' constant for MCWA from the beginning. Not only have they encouraged me from the start with this project but have kept me on course and made it all the sweeter. Besides all this, I am indebted to them for their years of leadership, friendship and fun that they have shone into my life. Y'all are awesome!

I am extremely grateful to Cheryl Yennie for her help in researching the MCWA archives to ensure that we kept to the facts of history. Her encouragement to keep going has been priceless. Thank you for going the extra mile each time that I threw another question at you. Thanks to Cheryl and Lyman and Marge Osborne for their contribution to the early details of the MCWA story.

Thank you to Danny and Frances Kennison for their major contribution and willingness to help in checking the details. I am so thankful for you and count it an honour to have served with you in Meskine. Yours was the first home I was welcomed into in Meskine and I have loved having you in my life.

Thank you to Bert and Debbie Oubre for inviting me to join the MCWA team in Meskine all those years ago. You changed my life forever and I am blessed to be a part of what you started. Thank you for your obedience in serving God in the hard places. Thank you, Bert, for sharing your heart, personal story and memories of the early years in establishing MCWA and Meskine Hospital. None of us would have had the privilege of this journey without your pace-setting.

I will always be so grateful for Dave and Patsy Alfors who have encouraged me, fed me, loved me, taught me to play games and kept us all on an even keel. Thank you for sharing life with me on this journey. Thank you for choosing to join our team when you could have gone to so many other places. Thank you for cheering me along with this book.

Members of the Meskine 'Bintu' gang have added their stories to this book, to whom I am extremely thankful. I hope I have done justice to your memories. Thank you to Jacqueline Koster, the one and only Yaapendo Meskine. What an honour it has been to learn from your example of service, love for Jesus, tireless enthusiasm for life . . . and love for chocolate, which, as we know, staves off depression. Thank you for sharing your memories. Huge thanks to Lesley Baigent for her help with some of the stories, for taking the time to get the details correct. How special it would have been to have had John's personal input; thank you for adding his unforgettable voice, Lesley. We look forward to being with him again one day. Thank you to Carsten Kretzschmar for his contribution, and to Ruth Mulligan who translated it for us. Also, many thanks to Sarah Ford for her precious story and to Rachel Picton for her help. Many thanks to the hospital leaders for shining a light on the hospital employees' perspective as I gathered information. There are so many others who could have contributed incredible memories but I leave it up to them to write their own stories.

As a complete novice to the book-writing world, I have been extremely grateful for the insight, direction and advice from others with more experience than myself. Firstly, thank you to all at Authentic Media for taking the time to even consider my proposal, let alone run with it. Thank you for all your help, support and encouragement in making this dream become a reality. Many thanks also to David Smith, my brother Sean, Liza Hoeksma, Jane Fucella, Debbie Root, Len Woods and Tony Collins for their advice along the way. Thanks to those who were willing to read my first drafts and help me to sort out the mess.

The only reason that I have been able to be in Cameroon for so long is because of the selfless support, commitment and prayers of others. There are so many but I especially want to shout out a huge thank you to these people who have stood by me for so many years: Sally Gurney Knight, Heather Holgate, Kristina Drew, Graham and Chriss Batchelor, Pat Daly, Mollie Clark, Cyril Coventry, Tony and Margaret Pitkethly, Michael and Frances Clark, Barry and Bunny Kirk, Mark and Ann Penson, Sam Duncan, Paul and Emma Jennings, Charles and

Eleanor Mitchell, Ron and Jean Sprouse, Pam Allen, Colin Haughton, John and Jean Tidmarsh, Carol Runnalls, Brian and Val Shearer, Tim and Carolann Bunce, Richard Bird, Michael and Maureen McCabe, John and Jan Dean.

There have also been several churches and groups in the UK who have held Meskine Hospital in their hearts and my team along with it. Thank you to St John's in Weymouth, Bishopsgate Evangelical Church, Bessecarr Evangelical Church, Woodley Baptist Church, Beacon Baptist Church in Kilmington, and the prayer groups in Guildford, Grove, and Worthing. My home church of St Barnabas in North Finchley, London has been my strength and stay for most of my adult life and I am overwhelmed by the constant love and support that I get from this fabulous community. Thank you for staying with me for the long haul. Thank you to John and Anne Coles, Henry and Jane Kendal, and Colin Brookes for pastoring me so well. Thank you to all in the World Mission Support group at St Bs.

Thank you to the wonderful family of Pioneers UK who continue to support me and keep things going so well at HQ. Thank you to the MCWA family for adopting me as your own.

Besides all these people, there are those who have been influencers on my life, have invested in me, loved me, spoken plainly to me and shaped me into a better a person. My great chums Margaret Peach and Rosie Hughes have made my life a sweeter, funnier, more ridiculous experience – don't forget we are the normal ones! Thank you for keeping me grounded and in touch with where I have come from. Thank you to Margaret Adams, Susan Chalmers, Colin and Barbara Smith, Heather Peters and many other former missionaries who have understood the strange life that I lead and have encouraged me from their own experiences.

My deepest love and thanks goes to my extraordinary family. The 'family business' for us has been to carry the love of Jesus that we have experienced to those who have not. My parents, David and Theresa, taught my brother and I well to exist for the sake of Jesus and for others. Consequently, this has meant that I have lived a greater part my life away from them, but they have never complained or expected anything different from the path that I have followed. Their patience, love, constant encouragement, understanding, endless trips to the airport, putting up with my junk, and carrying the burden of the Fulbe with me has been a priceless treasure. I am honoured, proud and blessed to be your daughter. My big brother, Sean, continues to be the one I look up to. I love the way he loves Jesus, the way he loves his family, the way he loves those who have lost their way in life. You will always be my pace setter, Bruv. Sean and my fantastic sister-in-law, Jayne, have given me honour in Meskine by making me the proudest Aunty to the Fab 4. My wonderful niece and three incredible nephews have enabled me to have the esteemed title in Meskine of 'Googo'! I love you all to bits.

To my parents, brother, sister-in-law, nephews and niece, who have loved me greatly and allowed me to be away so much. Thank you for always welcoming me home again.

And to my Cameroon family, Scott and Lee, Dave and Patsy, my *Hama'en* and *Adda'en*. Thank you for making every day a Saturday.

1

What Happens When Terrorists Move In

I wearily wheeled my luggage over to the check-in desk and waited for the rather grumpy-looking attendant to look up to acknowledge my presence. He did not but gestured for me to hand over my ticket and passport. As I hauled my case up onto the scales I noted that it only weighed 15 kilos, so it was well under the limit. It was always lighter when I was leaving Cameroon as there never seemed to be much need to take stuff home. Coming from the UK to Cameroon, though, was a different story, and then my 46-kilo limit never seemed to be enough. This trip home, however, felt so different to all the previous ones. Usually my case would mostly contain gifts for family and friends, but this time I was in a hurry and ill-prepared, so I had stuffed in the essentials that I needed for the trip and a few other things that I definitely didn't want to lose if my house was looted during my absence.

I wasn't due home for another ten months, so my heart wasn't ready to leave my friends in Cameroon; in all the rush and stress, I hadn't even been able to say goodbye to them. My heart was sad and my mind was racing with thoughts, flitting from one thing to the next. I was glad that the check-in attendant didn't want a conversation, as I could hardly articulate anything. The weary, yet preoccupied, expression on faces of my team-mates and all the other foreigners in the airport that day told the same story. We had to leave Cameroon, but we did not want to. Circumstances beyond our control had changed the course of our lives forever.

The reason for all this upheaval and emotion was the activity of terrorists in our corner of the world, and their ruthlessness in seeking out and taking hostages, preferably foreign ones like us. By 2014 we had become their target and our presence was putting our Cameroonian friends in danger. We hoped it would be a temporary separation, but as we stepped onto the plane that day we had no idea if we would be seeing northern Cameroon again. After all our years of developing the medical project that had become Meskine Hospital, was this going to be the last time we stood in the place that had become home? Was this the last time we were going to see the faces of our beloved colleagues, those we had invested our lives in? Was this unpredictable threat to stability going to bring loss of life to our friends? And what about the hospital itself? Would the workforce be able to continue without the presence of the founders?

It all felt rather surreal and unbelievable to us. History had apparently been kind to Cameroon, with a rather seamless transition (compared to other countries) from the colonial powers to independence and then unification of the French and British regions of Cameroon. There had only ever been two presidents since that time, and peace was a pleasant state of being in this rather unsettled corner of Africa. Frequent ructions arose from the neighbours – Nigeria, Chad, Central African Republic (CAR) – but not in Cameroon. All seemed to be well. Being tucked up in the far north of a nation that rarely hit the international news radar, except for the occasional soccer match, we thought that the village of Meskine and its hospital were on a well-trodden path to a quiet life. But that changed when a group that became known as 'Boko Haram'[1] began its menace across the border in Nigeria, and was set to spill over into the surrounding countries, which put our region in its sights. This frightening scenario had been the furthest from my mind when I had first set foot in Cameroon many years before.

Africa had always been a curiosity to me when I was growing up in the UK. My father had travelled there several times in his capacity as an evangelist, and there had been some missionaries from our church who turned up from time to time with their exotic African stories. Occasionally my parents invited visitors from Africa to our family home, which made me wonder what life was like in this faraway place, but I never really thought I would end up spending a considerable chunk of my life there one day.

My big brother and I were brought up to know and love Jesus by our parents, but it wasn't until I was 17 years old that I really understood that there were still people in the world who had not had the opportunity to hear about him as I had. At that time I didn't recognize that God was calling me to 'become a missionary', which would later lead me to Cameroon; I was simply responding to the fact that I had understood Jesus loved everyone but not everyone had the opportunity to discover his love. At that tender age, I made a commitment to God that he could use me if he wanted to, to get the news of Jesus to others. By the time I was in my mid-twenties and working as a physiotherapist in London, I realized that the commitment I had made years before had still not been fulfilled. This realization was the fruit of a deeper work that God was doing in my life at that time as he helped me to get my priorities into an order that gave him space to use me. There was a growing desire in me to go somewhere beyond the UK, but in my heart, I did not want to go to Africa or to Muslims, rather preferring the beautiful mountains of Nepal or South America!

After much prayer and discussion with my church leaders, parents and friends, I contacted mission organizations, keeping an open heart and mind as to location and role. Should I offer to serve as a physiotherapist? Or as a church-planter? Or something else? After eighteen months of research and one application to a project in Chad, which mysteriously got lost, my mother discovered at a conference that Medical Centers of West Africa (MCWA) was looking for a physiotherapist in Cameroon. The UK-based organization Action Partners had advertised the position on behalf of MCWA so I contacted them to see what it was all about. It was advertised as 'Physiotherapist to set up a new physiotherapy department in a Christian hospital and join a church-planting team.' Finally, here was something that resonated with my heart. The challenge of setting up a new physiotherapy department plus work among an unreached people group[2] sounded very appealing to me and well worth investigating. I had no idea where Cameroon was, so I got a map out, discovering it was a neighbour to Chad, a country I had already been investigating. It was not long before the wheels were turning to get me to Meskine. I initially committed to eleven months of service in 1998, but it has since turned into a lifetime that I can only describe as pure privilege. The African sun has left its mark on my lined face, and I have learned to gradually lay down my agenda of marriage and motherhood, remaining contentedly single, much to the bemusement of my Cameroonian friends; yet, my heart is full of the exceptional honour of being a messenger of the love of Jesus to those who have not heard.

Hostage-Takings and Refugees

By 2013 my life and that of my team-mates in Meskine was about to take a dramatic turn as the terrorists began to cause fear, pain and destruction further inland in Cameroon. Our peaceful world was about to be rocked. There had been skirmishes and attacks on the border for some time, but the terrorists became bolder and, in their search for more resources and loot, began to move closer to more populated areas. Following this came their strategy to take foreign hostages, which finally made the Western media pay attention to the plight of this corner of the world. It also meant that foreigners in the area moved into higher alert, as the threat was becoming closer to home and more personal. It was no longer a security problem 'out there' but was creeping into our lives, our communities and our daily thoughts. The regular reports of more and more hostage-takings were very uncomfortable to hear.

The first foreign hostages to be taken were seven members of a French family, including children, in February 2013, followed a few months later by a French priest. In both cases it was assumed that a ransom was paid, as all were released after several weeks of captivity. By December 2013 our team members followed advice and were no longer travelling west and north of Meskine, as it was now evident that it was increasingly dangerous to do so. The single women on our team were recalled from living in the neighbourhoods to return to homes on the hospital grounds, where it was deemed to be safer; this included me, when I was living alone for a few days. Normally, I would be in the company of Dave and Patsy, my team-mates, as we shared a home together at this time, but their temporary absence meant I was more vulnerable, should our home be targeted. Calling us back to the hospital compound was an agonizing decision for our team leader, Scott, as the last thing he wanted to do was dictate to independent, rather determined women how to live. For us women it was a reminder that life was changing, as danger was looming not too far away.

From this time on, our team took increasing measures to improve security in our homes and at the hospital, not knowing how things would progress. We each had a 'safe room' built into our homes so that in the event of an attack to take us hostage we would at least have a reinforced room that would give us a short time to take refuge while we telephoned for help. We also kept a bag packed with clothes, passport and money, should we need to grab it and leave immediately. When I was out in public I remember becoming more conscious of not staying too close to the edge of the road if I was walking, and being more vigilant of vehicles slowing down as they approached me; it would, after all, only take a few seconds to be snatched into a car and whisked away. I had always been very conscious that my white skin meant that I could never 'blend in' while I was a visitor in Cameroon, but every time I went outside of my home now it felt as if I was deliberately drawing attention to myself, just by being there. It didn't matter how much I tried to cover up with a head covering and a veil – there was no hiding the fact that I was a foreigner as my white face, feet and forearms were always visible. It seemed to be a reflexive response of anyone that when I walked by they just had to shout '*Nasaara*', meaning 'white person'. Being invisible was not an option.

The situation around us in the region was gradually changing, too, in a spiral of events. The north-western town of Mora and surrounding area was becoming increasingly unstable, with frequent attacks. Being the nearest town to the border meant that many internally displaced people from Cameroon, and refugees from Nigeria, were flooding into it in an attempt to find a place of safety. The local churches were often the haven that was sought, but they soon became overwhelmed with the needs of these vulnerable people. A refugee camp was set up near the town of Mokolo for Nigerians who were flooding over the border to escape the violence; this became home to thousands.[3]

When two Italian priests and a Canadian nun were taken hostage in April 2014 a few miles north of us, it really did feel as though danger was getting too close to Meskine now. This capture happened around the same time as that of nearly three hundred schoolgirls from Chibok in Nigeria, leading to the 'Bring Back Our Girls' campaign, which was supported around the world and made global headlines. Our thoughts and conversations as a team and with other expatriates in the area were increasingly moving towards when, and no longer if, we should leave. It was at this time that the 24-hour armed military presence was taken on at Meskine Hospital to reinforce what our guards were already doing to keep the premises as safe as possible. The MCWA team began to reduce in size as short-termers left one by one, and we saw that the departure of all of us was now on the horizon.

The following month saw the biggest hostage-taking attack of foreigners to date in Cameroon when ten Chinese men, who had been working on road construction and repairs, were taken. Twelve vehicles and blasting materials were also snatched by the terrorists at the same time. Sadly, this was the first time they had killed someone in Cameroon in order to get non-Cameroonian hostages. The victim that day was a Cameroonian soldier. A line had now been crossed, which heralded the start of the exodus of foreigners from the far north region as it became more than clear that our very presence was now putting the population of Cameroon in danger. Boko Haram had shown that they would stop at nothing to get hostages. If a solider had been killed in the process of capturing the Chinese hostages, what would they do if they arrived at Meskine Hospital to take us? The thought of the lives of our friends and colleagues being put in danger because of our presence was extremely unsettling and, frankly, terrifying for us all. Consequently, events began to move quickly and by June 2014 we had left Meskine, leaving the hospital in the hands of our Cameroonian colleagues, having no idea how long we would be away or if it would be permanent.

Our departure had been abrupt as we did not announce that we were leaving. The reason for this was that some of the hostages who had previously been taken had made their departure plans known and it seems that they were snatched just before they had planned to leave. Was it timed to get them while they were known to still be there? We do not know, but we chose to keep our plans to ourselves for as long as we could. This meant that our departure was rushed and we were unable to go around to our friends to say goodbye, which added to the unsettled feeling and sadness that we were all carrying in our hearts. To those we could tell, it was heavy news and another reminder to them that their lives were changing forever. The uncertainty of what tomorrow and the rest of their lives would bring was etched on their faces and it was impossible to keep our emotions under control. As I returned to the UK, and my team colleagues went to the USA or further south in Cameroon, we left with heavy hearts, but all of us knew that it was the right decision; so did our friends in Meskine.

It was only after I had left that I realized how exhausting it had truly been to live in such tension and to have been in 'high alert' mode for so long. When I was finally back home in the

UK, it still took me a few weeks to calm down in my mind and realize that I could now relax. My team-mates reported a similar experience of feeling emotionally exhausted once they were at last in a safer place, but it didn't stop us from wondering how life was carrying on in Meskine without us.

Meanwhile, back on the frontline, besides all of these foreign hostages, there were hundreds of civilians being taken in Nigeria and Cameroon as the terrorists attacked and brutalized villagers, murdering and pillaging as they went. By mid-2018 it was estimated that more than 20,000 people had been killed by the group in the region since they started their military campaign a decade earlier.[4] A terrible horror story was unfolding that has led to many years of turmoil and heartbreak for thousands who have lost loved ones, livelihoods and homes, and become displaced. It can only be described as a catastrophe for Nigeria and the surrounding region and one that will take decades to recover from, if indeed, recovery is allowed to begin.

Changing Times

While we foreigners could leave in 2014, for the residents of Meskine and staff of the hospital it was a different reality. There were inevitable changes to their lives as the security situation in the region began to deteriorate. More stringent security measures were taken in schools, hospitals and churches, as suicide bombings were increasing in Nigeria. Inspections of bags, clothing and even Bibles were made in the search of hidden weapons and explosives. Going to the market or embarking on a journey was no longer a pleasure but rather a necessity that had to be endured; people would think twice before setting off now and would consider whether it was really a necessary trip.

There was heightened tension everywhere as suspicion grew of crowds, because you never knew who might be mingling there. There was the repeated conversation of shock and disbelief that all this sadness and tyranny could be going on right here on their doorstep. It did not take long for the northern economy of Cameroon to be drastically affected as market trading and transportation of stock became more challenging.

By the time we left the area there was increasing activity by the Cameroon military in the region as, for the first time in its history, Cameroon had declared war in an effort to defend itself. Military tanks and soldiers were becoming more visible on the streets as they mobilized towards the borders and set up control points on the roads. While we had still been there, it had given me an increasingly unsettled feeling as the loaded trucks of steely-faced soldiers and tanks thundered past on the roads. Curfews were set in place, prohibiting travel for all motorcycles between sunset and sunrise. It became mandatory for people to carry their identity cards with them everywhere they went in order to prove who they were, should they be stopped. There was an increasing suspicion and fear that terrorists were infiltrating the local population.

It turned out that my absence from Cameroon would be for six months, so by the end of 2014 I was able to rejoin my team-mates Scott and Lee, and Dave and Patsy, in the town of Ngaoundere. This location was a day's drive south of Meskine and was deemed to be far enough away from terrorist activity for us to stay in relative safety, while still being able to keep in contact with Meskine Hospital. It felt good to be together again as a team, hoping that we would be able to return to Meskine in the not-too-distant future.

By July 2015 it sadly became evident that Boko Haram activists had indeed made headway into the local population. This became apparent when three suicide bombers caused death and destruction in the central market area of Maroua, just 5 miles from Meskine. It seems that young women had either been recruited by the terrorist group, or had been forced somehow into putting on the explosive vests under their clothing and had walked into the crowds. It is not clear whether the women detonated the bombs themselves or if they were detonated remotely. The terror and destruction were instant; over thirty people were killed and many more injured. This was, however, hardly anything compared to the repetitive attacks that were happening in neighbouring Nigeria at the time, where hundreds more had lost their lives in a similar horrific manner.

When our team first heard the news of these bombings our hearts sank immediately. Had any of our friends been killed? Or injured? Was Meskine Hospital able to cope in a crisis like this? As news trickled in, it became clear that, thankfully, none of our close friends had been caught up in the attack, and most of the injured had been taken to hospitals closer to where the bombings had taken place; a few had been brought to Meskine where our staff had taken care of them admirably.

I later discovered that the husband of a friend of mine had been among those killed by the first bomb. He was a merchant at the main market in the town and had been sitting with his friends, drinking tea in the shade of trees at the time of the blast. Eyewitnesses of the event explained what had happened to his wife and family. A young woman, who was wearing the typical robes over her clothes and veil over her head, had a concealed explosive vest, but someone had noticed a flashing light. He shouted out, telling people to run, as he ran towards her to bring her down. At that moment the blast went off, tearing through the crowd. A horror scene of blood, body parts and mayhem was left behind. My friend's husband died instantly from his injuries, leaving his young widow to raise their children alone. On the other side of the same market on the same day, another suicide bomber detonated her bomb with similar devastating effects.

The third blast took place early one evening at a street-side bar. It was the busiest time as it was surrounded by restaurants and street-food vendors. It was still bustling despite the two bombs that had gone off three days earlier across the other side of the bridge that straddles the wide river through the centre of town. Another friend told me that her teenage son was in the area when the bomb went off. Somehow he himself escaped injury, but he knew eleven of the people who were killed that night. How does anyone recover from an experience like that, to suddenly lose so many of your friends in such a horrible way?

These suicide bombings became a watershed moment in our team's thoughts. Up to that point, we had still held on to the idea that it would be possible to return to Meskine in some capacity. It had still seemed possible that the coalition forces and governments could win the battle to restore security sooner rather than later. In our hearts we wanted it to be true, but these explosions in 'our' neighbourhood of Maroua finally showed us that this chapter in Cameroon's story would not be ending as quickly as we had hoped. We now realized that our lives and ministry base had been changed for more than a few months and that returning to Meskine to live would not be possible for a long time, if ever. For all of us it was a deep sadness, as we recognized that these bombing attacks had made our suspicions become a reality. The town of Ngaoundere had become our new home and we had to let go of the idea of returning long-term to Meskine any time soon.

Leaders for the Challenge

While we were adjusting to our new life further south and trying to refocus on our ministry roles there, Meskine Hospital
was growing up without us. Despite all this sadness, as time
went by it became evident that the departure of the missionary team had become a catalyst for the leaders of the hospital
to grow in skill and teamwork. A leadership team comprising
the administrator, the medical coordinator and the head doctor had existed since 2003,[5] but this was the first time they
had to lead without their mentors being nearby. They worked
together, along with all the department heads, to keep things
functioning each day. Regular communication with Scott and
Lee was still happening by phone, and later intermittent visits
from us of a few days at a time to Meskine ensured that encouragement and accountability were maintained. It was untested
territory for the local leadership team to run the hospital on
its own, so MCWA HQ in the USA and those of us on the
missionary team in Cameroon prayed and waited to see what
the outcome would be. Would the hospital leaders be able to
carry such a heavy responsibility in such testing times? Would
the end result be success or failure for this still rather young
hospital? Much to everyone's joy and relief it soon became very
apparent that they were more than capable as they all stepped
up their efforts and pulled together to ensure that it was 'business as usual' at Meskine Hospital.

All the years of training and working together with hundreds
of visiting medical volunteers were now bearing fruit as the
MCWA protégés of years past had grown up to meet this challenge head on. I had already experienced this pride and relief

in seeing my own physiotherapy colleagues, who I had trained, take over the leadership of the physiotherapy department a couple of years earlier. It's an incredibly satisfying feeling to know that all your years of pouring knowledge and encouragement into people will bear long-lasting fruit, benefiting others for years to come.

The maturity of the hospital team in Meskine was affirmed on several occasions when the conflict was particularly fierce on the border between Nigeria and Cameroon in 2016. Both the Nigerian and Cameroonian Governments sent delegates to thank and encourage the hospital staff for their dedicated hard work during times of conflict. Meskine Hospital had come to their attention as it became the first choice for emergency medical care for injured military personnel, prior to their being transferred to military medical facilities in the south of Cameroon. This was a huge boost to the morale of the hospital staff just at a time when they needed it. They were working so hard with so many urgent cases, many of which were horrific injuries caused by mines and other explosive devices. Sometimes it felt as if they were working with no end in sight, but there was a sense that they were serving their country by serving the injured military coming through their door. They knew they were doing their part for the greater good in a time of war, and nothing could have made us feel prouder of them at that moment. During one of our short visits at this time we found a genuine sense of the hospital staff becoming a stronger community than ever before, standing together in service to their patients. They wanted people to know that, no matter what, they would still provide the good quality medical care that Meskine Hospital had become known for.

Because of the conflict situation, there was a small American military presence in the region who also got to know of Meskine

Hospital. Recognizing the importance of the facility for the region at this time, they offered to help by training our staff further, specifically to set up a triage system[6] for dealing with mass casualties. A hangar (a roofed, open-sided structure) at the back of the grounds was chosen as the reception area where large numbers of patients could be organized into priority for care, should the need arise. We ourselves had the privilege of taking part in and witnessing a training exercise of a mock mass casualty influx in 2016 during one of our visits; it was very clear that this special training had been taken on board and added to the skills of the hospital team. Watching our friends and colleagues of many years move into this maturity and level of effectiveness in a highly charged situation was extremely encouraging for us, confirming that God had the running of the hospital in his hands, even in times of war. This training for dealing with mass injuries was needed and put into practice on several occasions when the conflict was at its height that year.

Another encouragement came in the form of *Médecins Sans Frontières* (Doctors Without Borders) and the Red Cross. These two organizations exist to give support in zones of conflict, so it was no surprise that they came to northern Cameroon at this time. When they arrive in an area they evaluate what medical facilities are already present and could benefit from being further supported and developed. In this capacity they visited Meskine Hospital. As they toured our facility and talked with the leadership team, it became apparent that they were not used to seeing such a well-functioning hospital in this part of the world in these circumstances, and they applauded the hospital's efforts.

To a certain degree, the unrest and security around the region began to calm down in the years following 2016. Life got back to normal, the markets functioned again, the night-time curfews were relaxed and there were fewer roadblocks in the vicinity. The news in Nigeria and around the border into Cameroon told a different story though. At the time of writing, terrorists are very much still present and intent on causing chaos and the people living there know it. Our friends in Meskine know that the peace of today may not be there tomorrow. It is still not possible for foreigners to live safely in the area, as the threat of being taken hostage remains.

If this security situation had existed a few decades earlier when MCWA was being formed and the vision for Meskine Hospital taking shape, it is certain that it would never even have got off the ground. The situation back then was thankfully much more peaceful, which ensured that this little Christian hospital in the village of Meskine, tucked up in the far north of Cameroon where Muslims dominated the culture, could be born. It was the result of a seed planted in the mind of a man gripped by Jesus, thousands of miles away in the deep south of another country, on the other side of the ocean.

2

From the Deep South to the Far North

Back in 1997 when I was first put in contact with Bert
Oubre and Lee Pyles from MCWA and considering coming
to Meskine to start up the physiotherapy work, I was rather
bemused to discover that the origins of this project all came
out of Baton Rouge, Louisiana.[1] I am from the south-eastern
corner of England but I have travelled around the world a little
bit; I had even lived in the USA for a year as a child, when my
father's ministry as an evangelist took us there as a family. But –
forgive me, readers from the USA – I could not place where
Baton Rouge was on the map, and even struggled to pinpoint
Louisiana. Of course, my education has now progressed, and
I have even had the privilege of visiting there, but at the time
it rather surprised me that a team from the Deep South of
America had ended up in the far north of Cameroon.

Baton Rouge, Louisiana, is indeed a special place. That it
is the home of the Louisiana State University (LSU) Tigers
football team was the first thing I learned about it from my
new friends when I got to Meskine. The purple and yellow
colours of the beloved team had been carried across the ocean
and the desert, establishing a fan base there. Over years of rub-
bing shoulders with my dear friends I have learned that their
home is so much more than this though: gumbo, crawfish and

jambalaya; swamps, searing heat, crepe myrtle trees and hurri-
canes; old plantation homes telling of days gone by; the curi-
ously enchanting Cajun accent and the ample indications that
the French have made their mark. A warm welcome is guaranteed and hospitality flows as steadily as the mighty Mississippi
River. And don't forget the Tabasco sauce and the Tony's sea-
soning on the table. Welcome to Baton Rouge, y'all!

It was out of this place that MCWA was born and set up its
headquarters. The journey from Baton Rouge to Meskine will
take you a couple of days on several aeroplanes but the development of MCWA was the cumulation of the spiritual journeys
of a number of people, beginning with Dr Bert Oubre.

Bert Oubre was born in Louisiana and was raised to go to
church, but as he left home, got married, started a family and
pursued his studies, church and Jesus were no longer a part of
his life. He attended LSU, where he trained to become a doctor,
but his conversion to Christ in mid-life while working as a very
successful general surgeon in California meant an unexpected
change of direction for him. When his wife, Alayne, was dying
with cancer at the young age of forty-two, feeling totally helpless
Bert became obsessed with needing to know whether there was
a heaven and a hell, and if so where his beloved wife was going.

Over three days, while driving between the hospital and
home, something rather bizarre happened. He never listened to
Christian radio but each day, when he drove, the same Christian station was tuned in. The first two times he changed it
back to his usual pop station but the third time he left it on
the Christian station and listened to the Bible teachers featured. For the first time in many years Bert's heart was turning
towards Jesus again. For the next six months while he took
care of his ailing wife, Bert started reading the Bible, beginning
at Genesis, forcing himself to read for several hours each day.

By the time he reached the New Testament he was looking forward to getting home to read and care for Alayne. Bert was especially impacted by the words of Jesus, becoming very aware of his own sin and need of a Saviour; as he read he discovered that the only one capable of saving someone's soul was Jesus Christ. Consequently, he put his trust in Christ, turning his life and future over to him; the next morning he awoke with inexplicable joy and profound peace. A few months later Alayne passed away but not before Bert was assured that she too was at peace with Jesus.

For this successful surgeon, his life was no longer to be centred on a settled prosperous life in the USA but to be uprooted to Africa. As Bert discovered a new life with Jesus as his Lord, it led him to World Medical Missions, investigating how he could use his surgical skills in mission hospitals overseas, which took him to Zaire in 1986. Here Bert met a young American-Swiss nurse named Debbie, who helped him out with understanding what was going on in this world of French speakers. Debbie's story was completely different, as she had grown up in French Guyana, where her parents had served as missionaries. Her facility in French was something that the rest of her future team-mates could only aspire to.

This time together turned out to be the beginning of the rest of their lives as, later that year, Bert and Debbie became engaged to be married. Immediately after their engagement, Bert made his first trip to Cameroon to Mbingo Baptist Hospital in the English-speaking north-west province to offer his surgical skills. It was here that he first met Fulbe people and he became increasingly aware that God was giving him a special interest in and love for them.

After Bert and Debbie were married in the USA at the end of 1986, they returned to Cameroon together to work at

Mbingo for a few months, where the vision for Meskine Hospital began to emerge. As Bert learned more about the Muslim Fulbe people and the need for good quality medical facilities in the far north province of Cameroon, where the Fulbe culture was dominant, the idea for Meskine Hospital was taking shape. They returned to the USA with this burning vision in their hearts and, being a man of great determination and courage, Bert soon set about raising support for the future project.

Being based in Baton Rouge when they returned to the USA and being members of the same church as Scott and Lee Pyles and Danny and Frances Kennison, God brought all their paths together in an extraordinary and perfectly timed way. These three families became the founding members of Meskine Hospital and the first missionaries sent out by the fledgling non-profit organization, MCWA, which was established in 1989. Their church, 'The Chapel', was also right behind them every step of the way.

Scott and Lee's story of how they got to Meskine was marked with a very specific calling to serve God among the unreached, which took them from their professional paths to that of pioneering missionaries. Both came to faith in Jesus aged fifteen; when they met at Louisiana Tech University they were both still maturing in their faith but discovering the absolute joy of bringing others to Jesus too. This was a trait that would never leave them and God was using this time to embed Jesus' calling to be disciple-makers. By the time they were married in 1985, Scott was successfully working in business management and Lee was a nurse at a local hospital. They were a typical young professional couple, starting out on the American Dream.

By the end of 1987 though, God had spoken to them both in various ways so that their priorities for life had completely changed. Scott and Lee made a commitment together, making themselves available for God to use in order that others would get an opportunity to hear about Jesus. They had no idea where this decision would lead them but assumed it would be a short-term trip somewhere, possibly Asia, for six months or so. Years later Lee would recall her thoughts as a 15-year-old when she had started her new life with Jesus, 'Lord, I'll follow you but please don't make me go to Africa . . .' It was at this time, as Scott and Lee were praying about where God would have them go in the world, that they were introduced to Bert and Debbie Oubre at their church. After hearing about the proposed project to start a medical work in Cameroon, God spoke very clearly to Scott late one night while he was praying. He knew without any doubt that God was calling him and Lee to join the Oubres in this venture, and not long after this Lee too knew that God was calling them, as she experienced extraordinary peace about the momentous decision.

Danny and Frances Kennison also underwent a complete turnaround in their lives as, within a few months in 1989, they responded to God calling them to join the Oubres and Pyles in this adventure with MCWA. Danny and Frances had both committed their lives to Jesus before their marriage and were getting on with their family life with Jesus at the centre. Danny had started a successful carpentry and house-building business while their family life became established in Baton Rouge. In the spring of 1989, however, a life-changing event happened for them when they attended a missions conference at their church. Listening to Don Richardson, a pioneer missionary to the jungles of Papua New Guinea, Danny and Frances began to understand from the Bible that God was a missionary God and has always desired all peoples and nations to know him. Danny gradually became convinced that God was calling him also to be involved in a significant way to reach the unreached. As he shared all this with Frances she realized that she was not in the same place of conviction about the idea as Danny. She prayed for God to change Danny's mind, but it was in fact her heart and mind that were changed, as God tenderly brought her to the point of hearing his call.

As the new MCWA team was making plans for how to get started in Cameroon, Danny learned of their need for a builder for the hospital. It seemed that God had prepared the Kennisons' hearts at just the right time in order for them to respond to this invitation to join the MCWA team.

After a survey trip to the far north of Cameroon in 1989, this newly formed MCWA family began to make preparations, with the help of Sudan United Mission (SUM) organization who were already involved in medical projects in the same area. They initially pursued building a hospital in the town of Bogo which was a known area for Fulbe, but when the papers came back from the Cameroonian Government they had surprisingly given permission for the new hospital to be built in the village of Meskine! To this day nobody knows why this change of location had occurred but it was an unchangeable decision; it seemed that God had a different plan.

After Bible seminary and French language studies, the three families and their children were finally all together in Cameroon in 1992 when the building of the hospital in Meskine began in earnest, under the direction of Danny. Bert Oubre was the medical director of the new hospital, with Debbie overseeing nursing and maternity care; Scott Pyles took on the role of hospital administrator, while Lee took on nursing and supplies management. Frances Kennison became the coordinator of home-schooling for all of their children at the 'Barefoot Academy' and later played a significant role in organizing the pharmacy.

Incredibly, by March 1995 after many months of hard work, Meskine Hospital was officially opened with a team of newly trained, young, enthusiastic nurses working in an outpatient department, on two wards, in a surgical room and a small laboratory. Things were up and running and it was not long before the increasing number of patients began to dictate the rapid rate of growth of the hospital facility. The initial plan of a modest thirty-bed hospital soon evolved beyond expectations as patients came from far and wide. Having a good quality surgical facility was a major attraction, and Meskine Hospital soon gained a good reputation for doing honest work at a decent price. The number of beds steadily increased to 130 at the busiest times. An X-ray and ultrasound department was soon added, and the physiotherapy department got going when I joined the team in 1998. A maternity ward, children's ward, private rooms, pharmacy building, administration block and extended workshops were all built as the need pushed the growth ever onwards.

The workload of the hospital was not being carried by these three families and new employees of the hospital alone though. Right from the outset, MCWA was keen to recruit short-term medical volunteers to come and help in any way they could, and to partner with other mission organizations. I am thankful for this foresight of MCWA to extend the invitation to workers from the UK, which has given me the privilege of working in Meskine all these years. I became part of the growing group of hundreds of other willing volunteers who came to Meskine to lend a hand. Words cannot express the enormous contribution that short-term volunteers to Meskine have made right from the beginning, whether they came for a few days or two years. Most would have called themselves simply 'spokes in the wheel' of MCWA's work. The reality was often so much more than this, though, as in the eyes of those they came to help they were like 'superheroes' flying in from all corners of the globe to save the day. They usually arrived at 'just the right moment' when the workload was becoming too much for the resident team to bear. So many doctors, surgeons and nurses came and filled the gap when no other medical expert was around; pharmacists, lab technicians, sonographers and X-ray technicians, teachers for the missionary children, medical equipment specialists, physiotherapists and occupational therapists, IT developers, accountants and electricians came willing to serve and do whatever was necessary to help. The indispensable visits of precious family and friends from home brought so much more than treats with them. They brought the sense of not being forgotten and being very much loved. God's perfect timing in bringing so many 'superheroes' to Meskine was a constant source of wonder to the MCWA team, and a reminder that God was in control.

The challenges presented to the MCWA team of building a hospital from scratch in a different culture far from home have been plentiful and varied. For Danny and the construction team the terrain itself turned out to be something to contend with from the outset. The clay soil with a topsoil of sand meant that nearly every building they constructed would develop fissures as the foundations moved subtly over time, thus requiring constant maintenance and repairs. The extremely hot, dry and dusty climate for most of the year has meant that medical supplies and equipment are often doomed to a much shorter lifespan than normally expected. Establishing the X-ray department led to extended frustration as it took so long to get an adequate electricity supply to the hospital to run the needed imaging machinery. Getting regular medical supplies to Meskine at an affordable price, finding and recruiting Cameroonian doctors willing to live in the hot dusty north, and learning to function within Cameroonian laws have all been part of an exhausting learning curve. But there have been certain nuances of life presented to us that particularly pertained to running a Christian hospital in a Muslim culture that have shaped the experience of all of us who have served there.

It is a well-known fact that Muslim cultures around the world reflect a certain modesty in dress for both men and women, and this was one of the first things I noticed when I arrived in Meskine. Fulbe men wear long robes reaching down below their knees over their trousers. You rarely see their arms exposed, or their heads without an embroidered hat. Fulbe women wear long, wrap skirts down to their ankles, with matching blouses and a head covering; over this there is a second wrapper or a veil draped around their heads and upper body. Some of the Muslim women also wear an extra black gown over these clothes, which is no mean feat in the extreme heat of the hot season. You can imagine the amount of undressing, or unwillingness to undress when it comes to medical assessments. In order to make a decent evaluation in physiotherapy, for example, you have to see and touch the body part that is causing the problem, so one of my first lessons was to explain why undressing was so important and that I wasn't simply going to prescribe some medication for the patient to take.

Being surrounded by this culture of modesty, I soon learned that the lives of men and women are very segregated among the Fulbe. They do not socialize together other than greetings or family occasions; they do not touch each other in public, even husbands and wives; they do not even eat together when they are at home. Direct eye contact between men and women during a conversation is also considered unseemly and rather brazen. So when a male patient is presented with a female doctor or therapist at the hospital and asked to take his clothes off it can come as rather an uncomfortable encounter for him! The same is also true for the women when presented with male medical workers. This awkward situation became part of getting used to working in Meskine, for me and my patients. After all, they came to us because they wanted to get better and if they had to pay the small price of immodesty for few minutes then most were willing to go with the flow. Just occasionally I would be faced with a man who refused to be touched by me and requested that my male colleague take charge. This would lead to a rather complicated scenario at times when I was still training my physiotherapy student, as I talked him through the assessment and treatment of the patient while I stood on the other side of the curtain!

An agonizing challenge that often presented itself to the medical staff, especially the surgical team, was the need for life-saving blood donations from family members. There was no local 'blood bank' to draw from, so when the urgent need arose it was up to the family members to offer themselves to help their suffering relative; but finding a willing donor was often like trying to catch hold of a vapour. The common mindset of the region was that it would be dangerous to give your own blood to someone else, that it would weaken you so much that you would also become ill, so better not to do it. There was simply no comprehension that giving a small amount of your blood would not be detrimental to your own health if you were healthy, and lengthy explanations from the medical team would often be fruitless. Not surprisingly, it was not uncommon to see visiting volunteers from overseas strung up to a blood bag somewhere, as they just could not bear to see another life needlessly lost.

Finding ourselves in a culture that had different opinions about the origins of illnesses proved to be a never-ending learning experience for us too. The Fulbe, along with all the other people groups of the region, have their own understanding of the causes and treatments of symptoms, especially those that do not seem to have an obvious physical manifestation. If there is no apparent wound or external sign on the body that something is wrong then it is often assumed that the cause cannot be physical but is, rather, spiritual; and therefore going to the hospital will not be sufficient. The general thought is that 'white man's medicine' is for physical illnesses such as infections, swellings, bleedings and pains, but if the problem is less obvious, for example epilepsy, infertility or hidden internal tumours, then Fulbe people tend to choose their traditional treatments first. Even physical problems brought to the hospital would often be 'helped along' with simultaneous 'treatment' that was surreptitiously continued when the doctor wasn't looking. We would often find amulets attached to the patient on their clothes, in their hair or around their neck; there would be visitors bringing a blackened liquid for the patient to drink which was the ink that had been washed off a wooden slate that qur'anic verses had been written on; sometimes we would find a visiting *marabout* (traditional healer) bringing some of his herbs or leaves for the patient, or a qur'anic teacher who would mumble some qur'anic verses and then gently spit over the patient. Generally these things are looked down on by those who claim to follow a purer form of Islam, but there was no escaping the fact that these were widely held traditions by the Fulbe, and in times of a health crisis they often instinctively called in as much help as possible.

Another area of care that presented confusion for us foreigners and patients alike was how to help those suffering with mental illness. Fulbe culture has a very vivid experience and understanding of the spiritual realm according to their traditions;

the presence of *ginnaaji*, or spirit beings, is a very active part of life. The understanding is that there are spiritual beings that can do good or harm to you that you can influence by how you live and how you treat them. This leads to the understanding that if your mental health is somehow altered then you must have done something to upset your *ginnaaji*, or someone else may have cursed you so that the *ginnaaji* are attacking you. Fulbe consider most mental illnesses to be untreatable by modern medicine and therefore tend not to bring these patients to the hospital for help, but when all other sources of traditional treatment have failed then the family finally tries the hospital to see if anything else is on offer. What may have been a relatively moderate case of depression, psychosis or schizophrenia has been left to simmer at home leading to much suffering for the patient and family alike, sometimes even leading to the embattled victim being chained by their ankle to a stake in the ground, to prevent them from harming themselves or others.

As we began to learn the culture and language of those we had come to live among, it became easier to understand the reasoning behind the decisions that people made, and the same was true for the employees we worked alongside. Our Cameroonian medical colleagues began to learn about the foreigner's mindset as we in turn learned from them. But something we often shared frustration with was the fatalistic Fulbe mindset of 'whatever happens is God's will' and therefore must be accepted and not questioned. It is true that there are some things that we as humans just cannot change, such as congenital illnesses, or forces of nature. But when not seeking treatment for your malnourished child or wife with breast cancer was also put into this category we found ourselves wrestling between trying to understand the culture and wanting to jump up and down with frustration. How could the family leave their loved one in this state for so long? If only they had come to the hospital earlier. Why bother coming now when it is too late? One could only conclude that the family too were not at peace with the situation being 'God's will' and hoped that the hospital might be able to do something after all. Sadly, the lateness of their arrival often fulfilled their own prophecy that it was God's will, as their loved one could not be helped, the illness being so far advanced.

There was one challenge of the culture, however, that loomed large and affected all of us every day as we went about our work. We could not escape the fact that we found ourselves living in the shadow and consequences of the Tower of Babel[2] as our brains, ears and tongues battled with a mixture of languages.

3

People from Many Tribes and Nations

As with all the medical team volunteers who have passed through Meskine, I came to a rather overwhelming conclusion very early on during my first days there. The ease of communication that I had taken for granted while being in my home culture was now long gone, and that would affect everything I did from now on. Take the assessment of one of my patients' needs, for example. In my home country of the UK I was used to having a short period of time, maybe twenty minutes on a good day, to evaluate what my patient required of me as their therapist. I discovered in Meskine, however, that after twenty minutes I was still only scratching the surface of what I needed to know.

Cameroon is officially French-speaking in the northern part, and I thought I had done quite well by learning some French before coming, but as I sat opposite the elderly man with my physiotherapy colleague, it was obvious that French was not going to be enough. I was thinking in English and talking in faltering French, wanting to know how long this man had been suffering from back pain. My colleague in turn translated my question into Fulfulde addressed to the son of the old man; the son then translated the question into their language of Tupuri. The answer to my question came back in the reverse order but was not very helpful in moving the assessment forwards. 'Yes, it's his back that hurts,' was the reply! I wiped the sweat from my forehead trying not to look exasperated, realizing that this assessment was going to take a long time, and tried asking the question again. This muddle with language was to become a very present part of normal daily life.

Incredibly, Cameroon with only a population of around twenty-five million manages to be home to approximately two hundred and fifty distinct ethnic groups and languages. Diversity seems to be very much a part of its identity. One end of the country is completely different to the other in terrain and climate, food and clothing, language and customs. As a visitor to the country and specifically to Meskine, it will not take you long to realize that one of the most overwhelming things about working here is the cocktail of languages that surround you and bombard you at every turn. Officially, Cameroon is a bilingual country using French and English, a constant reminder of its complicated colonial history. However in the far north region of the French-speaking part, English is virtually of no use at all and French is only useful if you are conversing with others who have been to school at least to the end of primary school-level education. This immediately rules out a large proportion of the rural and Muslim women, and a significant chunk of the men. In more recent years I have perceived that the habit of sending children to school has been increasing; I have also noticed that there seem to be more children attending school in the more prosperous south than in the far north of the country.

Because of this official use of French in the far north province, most foreigners who have come to work in Meskine for a significant period of time have tried to come with a certain functional level in the French language . . . only to discover on arrival that you will still be dependent on a translator to help get you through the day for a lot of the time! This is part of the ongoing lesson in humility that followed us through our Meskine experience. Local languages are obviously the first choice for most, but one language has come to dominate and become the first or second language of the majority; it is Fulfulde, the language of the Fulbe people.

When Bert Oubre and his team first had the vision to build Meskine Hospital, and MCWA was formed, it was the Fulbe people who grabbed their attention. The Fulbe, also known as Fulani, are a vast group of around thirty million people, spread across the Sahel of sub-Saharan Africa, traditionally nomadic, pastoral cattle-owners. From Senegal in the west to Sudan in the east, Fulbe have wandered over hundreds of years keeping their ethnic identity and traditions alive. Although there are distinct clans and dialects among them, there is the common thread of *Pulaaku*, or 'Fulbeness' that marks them out from other ethnic groups. Qualities of patience, controlling emotions and guarding a sense of 'shame' are highly valued.[1] There is also a distinct beauty in their appearance and a remarkable elegance. Their slender frames, big eyes, narrow noses and lips, and lightly hued skin set them apart, and they possess a way of moving that gives the impression they are never in a hurry or impulsive, even gliding above the ground somehow.

For hundreds of years the Fulbe have been Muslims and have been instrumental in the spread of Islam across Africa. The purity and strand of Islam that is followed though can vary enormously, depending on location and lifestyle. The Fulbe who have become more settled and live in towns and villages are more likely to follow a purer version of Islam, and be able to read the Qur'an for themselves; many will have been able to take part in the pilgrimage to Mecca and will be avid adherents to the other essential pillars of Islam, including fasting and praying. Conversely, it seems the further away Fulbe are from other communities and the more nomadic the lifestyle, then the less pure Muslim they will be. Rather, theirs will be a religion of syncretistic beliefs where amulets play an important role and the power of the Qur'an is actually in the physical writing down of the words rather than understanding what the words mean. So different is the culture between the 'bush Fulbe', sometimes referred to as 'Mbororo', and the 'town Fulbe' that there can be a real suspicion and antagonism between the two groups, even a fear. Many town Fulbe fear the perceived occult power of the bush Fulbe; many bush Fulbe look down on the town Fulbe for being 'sell-outs' to the non-pastoral lifestyle and mixed marriages with non-Fulbe.

Over decades and centuries in the far north of Cameroon there has been a very purposeful intermarrying of Fulbe with the non-Fulbe tribes in order to gain political and regional power, and also to advance the proliferation of Islam. When you ask Muslim people today in the region if they are Fulbe, the immediate answer will be, 'Yes, of course,' but on closer discussion it will become clear that one parent or two grandparents were actually from one of the hill tribes and converted to Islam when they married a Pullo (singular form of Fulbe); since this time the family connection to their pre-Islamic culture and identity will have become dislodged. To distinguish themselves from these mixed ethnic lines, a Pullo who is proud of his lineage will call himself a Pullo *maama joweedidi* – one who can count his pure Fulbe line back seven generations.

The population of Fulbe in Cameroon is not fully known but is estimated to be at least two million, mostly situated in the northern half of the country, but the diaspora spreads far and wide. Through land conquests and brutal battles, the Fulbe took over most of the chiefdoms from the indigenous tribes in the eighteenth and nineteenth centuries and continue to hold many of these positions today. This means that the Fulbe culture and language now dominate, so much so that Fulfulde, the language of the Fulbe, is the common trade language used by most in the northern sector of Cameroon. There is probably no other region in Africa where so many non-Fulbe people speak Fulfulde. Even the churches preach and sing in Fulfulde in northern Cameroon, as this is the common language for most people from different tribes. It is ironic that the language of the Fulbe has been used in so many Cameroonian churches since their earliest days, yet not even one person from the Fulbe nation has set foot in most of these gatherings. The most commonly used Bible in the northern churches is the Fulfulde Bible, but rarely will any Fulbe have set their hands on it, let alone read it.

So it was to these Fulbe people that MCWA came in 1992, spurred on by a burning vision to build a hospital to meet the physical and spiritual needs of these then 'unreached people'. It became clear to us that although there were several well-established denominations of the Christian church in this region, their focus of ministry had been the non-Muslim population and not the Fulbe. At the time of the hospital inception, there were one or two known Fulbe followers of Jesus but, frankly, the local church saw it as an almost impossible and worthless task to try to reach more.

The first MCWA team members quickly became used to providing an increasingly appreciated medical service as Meskine Hospital received patients from many different ethnic groups. Right from the outset, there were always many patients coming from the indigenous northern tribes of Guiziga, Tupuri, Mafa, Mufu, Mundang, Masa, Mousgoum and Kapsiki, to name but a few, and many of the initial hospital employees come from these groups. But the geographical position of the hospital is situated in the small 'head' of the Cameroon cockerel (if you look at a map of Cameroon it looks like the profile of a cockerel), so the borders of Nigeria and Chad are not that far away. Consequently, we would also find ourselves chatting with people from Hausa and Kanuri backgrounds, and others from Kotoko, Mandara and Arab Shuwa. In fact, there was a period from 2004 for a few years when there appeared to be more people in the hospital speaking Chadian Arabic, the language of neighbouring Chad, than any other language, to the extent that many of the employees seemed to learn the language overnight, leaving us visiting foreigners in awe and wonder.

It also occurred from time to time that people had travelled many days to come to Meskine Hospital: a week-long journey from Sudan; a nightmare of a road trip from the CAR; several plane tickets and taxis from Libya or the Arabian Gulf. Even some adventurers from the Cameroonian diaspora from Europe or elsewhere had made the journey back home. Many would hear about Meskine Hospital from their friends or relatives, so curiosity led them to pay a visit to see what we had to offer.

This multiethnic community gained another dimension when all the different Europeans, Americans and Australasians who have passed through Meskine were added. At the very beginning it was very much an American project, with all the team volunteers being united by their common connection to Louisiana, but MCWA saw the value of partnering with other mission agencies early on. Soon Action Partners (which became Pioneers UK) started to send people from the UK and Netherlands; VKTM (which became Sahel Life) from Germany; Pioneers Australia from Australia and New Zealand. Nursing students from France and Switzerland also came regularly for a time. The expat team life was therefore always an interesting cross-cultural experience in itself. The team language was mostly English, but at times when non-English speakers were present French would be used as the common language, so we would all muddle along together. When the team was blessed with real French speakers from France and Switzerland our ears were treated to the beautiful French that we all aspired to, as the subjunctive and conditional tenses just flowed so easily for them!

Having a mixed-up team from different corners of the earth, it was inevitable that there would be differences in eating habits and this often became a memorable experience as we shared together. The non-Brits learned about the wonders of Marmite and trifles, the non-Louisianians about the absolute necessity of gumbo, the non-Swiss about the fabulous fondue and raclette, and the non-Dutch about fragrant speculaas biscuits. Then there was the obvious debate over which was the best chocolate: Cadbury, the American Hershey's or Germany's Ritter Sport.

Alongside this multinational hospital team, Meskine became a popular choice for other overseas workers in Cameroon for their medical needs. There was always a sizeable team of Bible translators and their families in the region, and various other non-governmental agencies based in the nearby provincial town of Maroua attracted many foreign workers – Italian, Finnish, Swiss, German, Italian, Polish, Korean, Canadian. The far north has also been on the tourist route for visitors to Cameroon, with the unusual hills of the Rumsiki area and the National Wildlife Park in Waza, so it would not be surprising to see a bus-load of weary tourists arrive to receive much-needed treatment for their dehydration, malaria or dysentery.

With all these different people descending on this little hospital in the village from all directions, it became a miniature 'united nations' existence and a melting-pot of multiple cultures. The richest of the rich *alhadjis*[2] might be waiting in line next to the crumpled farmer from the hills; the shy, veiled young mother, dressed head to toe in black, next to the bejewelled office worker in her shiny shoes and short skirt; the nomadic Fulbe family, wandering around the hospital wondering where to go and who to see, being directed by the arm-waving American; the aggressive Chadian being calmed by the easy-going Cameroonian; the pale tourist awaiting his malaria results next to the toddler who lived in the neighbourhood on the other side of the hospital walls.

In the early days of the emerging medical work, it would hardly have seemed possible that so many people from so many different tribes, nations and cultures would descend on this little place. It has in many ways become a crossroads where the world has met, and God himself has been among us all every day, drawing us to each other, helping us to love the other, opening our eyes to those who are different to ourselves and loving the wonder that we discover. It has not been without its challenges. Confrontations and misunderstandings have certainly been evident, adding to the colour of any experience in Meskine, whether it be as a patient, a member of staff or a visitor. But the handshakes and smiles have never been far away. Thankfully these simple actions are not bound by culture or language and are universally understood as, 'It's good to be with you, my friend.'

Once a visitor to Meskine from another culture has got over the shock of being plunged into this new way of life and language, there is a whole new medical community to discover, a 'world within a world' that has its own rhythm and pulse. Your first wander through Meskine Hospital is certainly a special experience of sights, sounds and smells that confirms you are a stranger in a strange land. Being here is a privilege, but getting here in the first place is not for the faint-hearted, as I was to find out.

4

Seeing the Hospital for the First Time

If you are fortunate enough to be one who has visited Meskine, you will not have forgotten your first trip. The impact of it will have had such a big effect on you. The story of your visit will have been etched on your mind, and you will tell and retell it for the rest of your life. My first visit in 1998 was no exception. This was my first foray into sub-Saharan Africa, my first solo trip, my first separation from home of more than a couple of months, my first cross-cultural physiotherapy adventure, my first efforts to obey God's call to serve in Meskine and what turned out to be the first of many more trips to this hot, dusty corner of Africa.

Physically getting to Meskine itself is usually unforgettable. International travellers arrive in the south of the country via the steaming port city of Douala, or the more bearable option of the capital city, Yaounde. In Douala the heavy, damp air greets you as you exit the plane and the distinctive smell of tropical Africa, mixed with sweaty bodies and plane fuel, fills your nostrils. What awaits you is the rather chaotic passage through immigration and baggage reclaim, often compared to a descent into madness. The area for baggage reclaim is simply too small for the volume of traffic going through it, so getting your feet stamped on and your ribs jabbed is to be expected.

Once you have miraculously found your baggage you are then forced to exit through a single door, with the crowd being funnelled past the hard stares of the customs officers. Once you have made it outside you are then faced with a throng of porters, taxi-drivers, currency exchangers, and sellers of mobile-phone cards, all clamouring for your attention and custom. By now you are drenched with sweat and all you want to do is sit down in front of a fan in a quiet room with a cold drink! The pace, temperature and chaos is mercifully much more manageable in Yaounde.

As Meskine is so far north, another journey is required. Taking the two-hour flight from the south to the north is the preferable route if the planes are flying that day, compared to an uncomfortable, bumpy, drive of two days. A Cameroonian bus trip of any length is only for the bravest, most adventurous of travellers, and my experience has led to me to avoid it as much as possible. As you bask in your good fortune of having a plane ticket for a flight that has actually taken off and is heading to your desired destination, looking out of the plane window you will notice that the verdant tropical landscape gives way to dusty brown savannah as you fly further north. The seemingly endless unoccupied space reminds you that this is a country with so much potential for growth and development. As you approach Maroua airport, the undulating hills to the north greet you as well as 'Mindif's tooth' to the east: a molar-shaped rock looking rather lonely in the vast expanse of bush land. The airport is a modest concrete box, containing smaller boxes of halls and rooms, built in the 1990s. Nowadays it seems rather tired and unloved but still functions adequately and keeps the air traffic flowing, so long as it's not dusty season when the thick dust clouds rolling down from the Sahara often bring the air traffic to a halt.

My initial feeling on arriving in Meskine for the first time was very much a sense of relief. I was finally here after months of planning. It was actually real and happening! I was greeted by the sweetest leg hug from cute little Jessica Pyles, who was nearly 4 years old at the time, and I remember feeling so welcomed by this team of strangers who would develop into dear friends and surrogate family. As I was driven out of the airport by my new team-mate Lee, the dust and the dry heat was the first sensation, mingled with the sweat as it trickled down my face. When I could finally stop thinking about this, I could not get over the fact that there were little homes made out of mud all along the side of the road. For some reason I was not expecting this at all but here it was in front of me – Cameroonians were still living in houses made of mud, and some still had dry grass roofs. Even now, over twenty years later, this is still a reality for many people.

The main village of Meskine consists of around 15,000 people, sprawled over 5 kilometres in length and about 2 kilometres in breadth. There is a meandering river on the south side that is dry most of the year but flows during the rains for two months. You will find well-established mango orchards and vegetable gardens planted all along the banks of this river most of the year round. To the north and west there are extensive expanses of fields, mostly used for planting the staple grains of millet and corn. To the east is the provincial town of Maroua, with a current recorded population of around 320,000 people,[1] but the reality is probably a lot higher than this. Over the years we have witnessed the joining up of Meskine to Maroua as the boom in house building continues. This is definitely a region of population growth.

Twenty-five years ago, the Fulbe chief of Meskine gifted MCWA a parcel of land to the north of the village, next to a little forest of neem trees. It was thought to be useless land with unproductive soil. It was here that a vision of a general hospital to meet the needs of the local population became a reality; the hospital compound is now a well-established, bustling community of activity and care.

As you approach the hospital today you will find a busy market area opposite the entrance where you can find breakfast, lunch and supper and almost anything else you might need to take care of your patient. If you can't find it here then you can wander down the path to the main market for about ten minutes and find it there. The smells of roasting meat, onions and spiced tea, mixed with smoke from the cooking fires, fills the air. In front of the restaurants and merchants are the motorcycle-taxi men, locally known as the *clondos*. For around US$1 you can travel to Maroua as a passenger; the more people and luggage you travel with will put the price up, though. It has been known to see whole families of five or six travelling like this on one motorcycle. More commonly you will see the driver with two passengers, plus their wrapped bundle of luggage placed in front on the fuel tank. Also at the front of the hospital is the parking area for visiting motorcycles and cars, all carefully monitored by the uniformed parking attendant. To the east side of the entrance is the mosque where locals and visitors meet together for the five-times-a-day prayers.

The hospital has a large rolling gate at the entrance that is opened in the early morning and closed in the evening. When open, there is a drop-down barrier that is monitored by a team of guards in their smart uniforms. They also keep a close eye on all who enter the hospital compound. The terrorist activity of the last few years has meant a step-up in security measures from years past; it is now necessary to use metal-detecting equipment to rule out explosive devices and arms being secretly brought onto hospital grounds. To boost the security there is also an armed military presence at the entrance, night and day. There is a plaque on the entrance wall announcing in French and Fulfulde that this hospital is God's space and for his glory: 'I will say of the Lord, "He is my refuge and my fortress, my God, in whom I trust"' (Ps. 91:2).

As you enter you will notice the well-kept plants, trees and flowers that, despite the dryness of the Sahel, are kept watered and therefore stay green all year round, giving a brightness to the scene. The multiple neem trees give much appreciated shade from the ferocious sun and there are large water jars under the trees inside for the benefit of all; the harsh heat means it is a well-used facility, as thirst is a constant companion here in hot season.

To the right as you enter is the *Salle de Conférence*, the meeting room. Staff meetings, training lectures, celebrations, hellos and goodbyes have been made over the years in this faithful building, often bursting at the seams as the staff team has outgrown it. Early morning prayers are held here at 6:45 a.m. to commit the day into God's hands and to ask for guidance. At 7 a.m. the staff start the new day, the new shifts begin, the departments are opened and the bustle wakes up again. Patients may have been waiting and camping out overnight to be first in the queue to be seen at the outpatient clinic in the morning, so there is always someone to see at 7 a.m. The gates are opened, the queue moves in, medical note booklets are bought and registered and the patients are directed to the 'vital signs' measuring room and then the consulting rooms. It won't be long before they are redirected to the lab for blood tests, to radiography for ultrasounds and X-rays, to the operating rooms for further consultation, to the tuberculosis (TB) specialist, or physiotherapy. If the patient is seriously ill, requiring immediate care, then they will be sent directly to the wards for admission.

There are now one hundred and twenty beds for inpatients on five wards, divided between men, women, children, maternity and isolation wards, but at times this has swelled to one hundred and thirty beds, depending on need. The wooden bed frames are rather tightly packed together these days to fit in the maximum number of patients. Some will have mosquito nets fitted up, others will have fans plugged in and positioned towards the patient. There will be plastic mats on the ground next to the beds where relatives make a space to receive visitors and look after their loved one. The under-the-bed space will be stocked with all kinds of foodstuffs, thermoses of tea and porridge, water bottles, clothes, bowls, and occasionally a live chicken awaiting its doom. Taking care of a patient is a rather full-time job for the families, as it is customary in Cameroon for them to do all the patient care apart from administering medicines and dressing wounds.

There will be a steady flow of visitors as people come to greet the patient throughout their stay, also bringing gifts of food; consequently, there can be rather a lot of bowls around at the end of the day. There is a hubbub of noise during visiting times as people circulate around the beds greeting, shaking hands, bowing in deference to their elders, squatting down to chat – not only with the patient they know, but also with the other patients they have never met, such is the importance of greeting the sick in Cameroon. The ceiling fans above their heads will be spinning faithfully, trying to circulate the hot air to make it a bit more bearable for all, the whirring and clattering adding to the noise. But when it comes to doctors' rounds all visitors leave, the ward doors are locked and a calm, settled air descends as peace resumes.

As you wander between the wards and other department buildings, you will notice groups of people huddled on mats spread out on the sandy ground under trees, surrounded by their bundles of belongings, pots, pans, food and bedding. These are the relatives of patients, who stay to take care of them. They are not allocated a bed on the ward but set up home outside, either under the trees or under one of the hangars in the grounds. Much of the year the temperature is so hot that most people are used to sleeping in the open air, so this is not unusual. As dusk falls, the outside parts of the hospital resemble a refugee camp, with mosquito nets being attached to any available tree branch, window frame or newly erected post in the sand and a sea of humanity dozing under the stars. Little kerosene lamps and battery lights mark out the more distant groups from the ones lit by the strip lights of the buildings.

During the daytime, in the midst of the activity there are toddlers and children wandering around, having the time of their lives as they explore this world of people. There is a great sense of living in community, especially if your sick loved one has to stay at the hospital for an extended period of time; your children become shared by the community, the hospital staff and the other families. Lifelong friendships are made here as you travel the road of caring for your loved ones together and your children growing up in this sub-culture away from home; sorrows and joys are shared, the trips to the market, the paying of medical bills, the daily laundry and the cooking all walked through together. Helping out with other people's children is a normal reflex for many of the visitors, and the children themselves soon learn to feel quite at home in this rather public situation.

The other noticeable groups of people that you will see during the working day are those who are waiting. Waiting is a

necessary part of any hospital visit. Waiting for your consultation, waiting for your laboratory results, waiting for your
X-ray, waiting for your loved one to come out of surgery, waiting to collect your pharmacy order, waiting for a baby to be
born, waiting for the vehicle to take your deceased loved one
away. But there is no clamouring – rarely is there any pushing or shouting. There is simply a patience, a calmness, albeit
disguising a suppressed frustration at times. Waiting is a part
of life, a skill that is learned from an early age and exercised
daily. But even the waiting becomes a sociable occasion here,
creating more time for greetings and chatting, for exchanging
stories and even a snack together. A fried bean cake bought for
your child, to keep them quiet while they wait, will be willingly
shared with your fellow-waiter's child.

The rhythm of the hospital day becomes obvious after you
have been here a little while. The early dawn is the start for
patients and their families. The first call of the mosque is heard,
the nurses do the first observations of the day, the outside bedding is put away, the mosquito nets are untied and folded up.
Then the 7 a.m. day staff start arriving, the morning prayer
time and devotions done, the departments open their doors and
the crowds start their journey through the consultations. The
doctors do their rounds, the nurses administer drugs and dress
wounds, the list for operations that day is worked through, TB
patients come for their monthly check-up, HIV patients come
for their monthly drugs, the physiotherapy department puts
people through their paces, the workshops build and repair,
the laundry is done again, the cleaners sweep and mop, the
admin team troubleshoots and organizes, the maintenance
team reacts to emergency building repairs. If it is the day for
pre-natal or post-natal clinics in the maternity block then there
will be an extra bubble of activity as the expectant and new

mothers gather, waiting for their turn and rather enjoying this opportunity to meet each other. The hub of life that is Meskine Hospital moves through the day like a finely oiled machine, and as 3 p.m. approaches, there is the glimpse of another day's work well done, people served and God glorified.

If you wander towards the back of the hospital where the workshops are you will find a quiet room, stacked with rejected and broken machines, tools and medical equipment. This is a room of miracles where a self-taught electrician from Meskine resurrects and repairs crucial items that keep the medical service running. Many times he has reinstated an important tool or machine by the skill of his hands as he calmly and methodically discovered the problem, and found a way to fix it. It seems that God has gifted this man in just the right way as replacement parts and equipment are so hard to come by here.

With all this activity going on, you would be forgiven for missing a team of two other men quietly making their way around the beds, visiting patients, and chatting with their families outside, or receiving people in their little office. These are the *aumôniers*, the chaplains, who take care of the needs of many who come through the hospital gates, by offering to pray, giving a word of encouragement, helping to meet physical needs whether it be a meal to eat or a mat to sleep on, detecting if someone is so poor that they can't afford to pay their bills and becoming their advocate, or offering spiritual guidance in a journey towards God. This is what the average day of the *aumônier* looks like, but it doesn't end at 3 p.m. Often they will be at the hospital into the evenings and even the night-time, following up on visits and offering a hand when people are in distress or when a loved one has died. Then there are the joys of being able to baptize people when they receive Jesus for the first time; or celebrating wonderful answers to prayer when people

are healed, and the long-awaited home-going of others who
have been in hospital for months. Meskine Hospital would
not be the same without the steady, life-breathing work of the
aumôniers; to the community they are called the 'pastors', for
that is what they have become to many.

The evenings at the hospital can be some of the most special times. The action of the working day has subsided, and
a calmness descends. There will still be many visitors coming
and going in the early part of the evening, many having been
commissioned to bring the evening meal from home for their
family. If you look carefully you will find people simply enjoying being together, chatting, planning, relaxing and recovering
from the day. In years past, before the insecurity brought by
Boko Haram, one evening each week the well-known *Jesus* film
was projected onto a wall near the entrance of the hospital,
drawing crowds of people watching and listening intently to
the events of Jesus' life as recorded in the Gospel of Luke. Many
local children and young people saw it so many times that they
could quote nearly all of it, word for word! We also found that
the quietness of the evenings was often the best time to go and
sit with people, to get to know them, to find out if anyone was
looking to understand more about Jesus and the Bible. People
were more ready to chat and were more relaxed than during the
busy daytime. It was reminiscent of that precious conversation
that Jesus had with Nicodemus who came to him at night;[2]
there's something special about the quietness and covering of
darkness that softens hearts to be drawn to Jesus sometimes.

As the last evening visitors return home and the gates are
closed at the entrance at the end of another busy day, the loud-
est sound is now the cicadas chirping away while the owls gently hoot from the trees, with the heavy, sweet scent of the neem
blossom filling the cooler night air. Day after day, year after

year for twenty-five years, this has been the rhythm of life at Meskine Hospital.

There has been another very special activity in the life of this community that has opened the door for God to step down, to caress and transform the inconvenience and pain, the mundanity even, of staying here due to a medical crisis.

5

The Prayer Round

It was one of those times of the year when malaria seemed to be touching every family in the village. Consequently, the children's ward at the hospital was full with little victims of the disease. As Scott entered the ward and looked at the full beds, he was struck with the heaviness of the situation; every single bed had a very sick young child lying on it, seemingly at death's door. Malaria was taking its toll. He felt overwhelmed as he started to pray for them one by one, the sadness and despair of each family was tangible to him. Scott managed to pray for every family and sick child that evening, but he went home with a very heavy heart and feeling exhausted from the effort of praying for the healing of so many children and not seeing any great change in their condition. His expectation was that some of these children would be dead by the next day as they were so unwell. With some trepidation, Scott made his way back to the ward the following morning to see how many of the children had made it through the night. As he entered the ward and looked around, he was shocked to see the beaming smiles of the families who had been so solemn the night before. Children were sitting up on the beds! Families were bright and chatting! Every single child was markedly better and making a good recovery. As Scott went from bed to bed to greet people, the families were quick to thank him again for praying and attributed the wonderful improvement of their child to God's intervention. Malaria is not too difficult for God to heal and the prayer of faith in Jesus' name that Scott had offered for each child had opened the door for God to touch each one in a wonderful way that night.

At the beginning of the life of Meskine Hospital it was impossible to know exactly what would unfold and how the medical service would develop. It was certainly not imagined that the hospital would grow to such an extent and size, with such a turnover of patients, and to have such a wide-reaching influence. The day-to-day running of things was not pre-scribed but has gradually developed according to need and patient load. Foundations of integrity, compassion and sound medical knowledge and practice were laid, along with a desire to represent Christ to any and all who came, giving them an opportunity to respond to him and the gospel. As the num-ber of patients grew it became increasingly difficult for staff and volunteer workers to have the time to just sit and chat with patients and their families and, therefore, to have quality conversations.

By the time the hospital was in its fourth year, in 1998, as a way to remedy this situation and create an opportunity for people to hear the gospel more intentionally, it was suggested that we take the time to visit every patient and their family at least once a week with the offer of praying for healing in Jesus' name. The suggestion came out of the action of a Cameroonian doctor who was working with us at the time. He saw the need to pray more intently for the hospital work and the patients, so he and a number of other staff started to meet one evening each week to do this. After a little while they saw that it would be even more appropriate to go to the patients and offer prayer at each bedside on the wards. This quickly became established on Tuesday evenings and known as 'the prayer round', so much so that even people who had never been to Meskine Hospital before knew that this was what we do. There have even been people who have come to us for this reason alone, stating, 'I have heard that you pray to God for your patients, so this seems like the best place to come to be made well.'

Each Tuesday evening, after the sun had set and the first of the evening calls to prayer had finished at the neighbouring mosque, several members of the hospital staff would make their way to the *Salle de Conférence* just inside the hospital grounds, along with some of their wives. From the opposite direction some of the missionaries wandered over from their homes; the faint aroma of insect repellent was in the air as we prepared to be bombarded by the evening mosquitoes. Handshakes having been exchanged between everyone gathered, the group settled down on the wooden benches for a few minutes to pray and ask God to direct us as we planned to go to every patient, bed to bed on every ward, to invite them to ask for God's healing touch. The group was divided into pairs, making sure that there was at least one French or Fulfulde speaker per couple. Each little team was allocated a ward so that all one hundred and twenty patients would be covered. As the team fanned out over the hospital the nurses welcomed us onto the wards, and patients and families looked up wondering what warranted this evening invasion.

As I and my prayer partner approached the first of the long row of beds, all eyes were on us, attentive to what we were about to say. 'Good evening, *Baaba*,[1] how are you this evening?' I asked, followed by all the other routine questions that a true greeting entails, the answer to which is generally, 'Everything is fine.' As we looked at the elderly man lying on the bed with sweat beaded on his forehead and his son fanning him with a tired piece of cardboard, his expression did not exactly give the impression that he was completely fine. He looked uncomfortable with his intravenous drip, his catheter and a big dressing over his abdominal wound having just had an operation the previous day. But he greeted us with a big smile, as did his family gathered around the bed. You could see the thought as it flashed into their minds, 'These visitors must be the doctors, surely, but why aren't they wearing white coats?'

To put their minds at rest, we explained the reason for our visit. '*Baaba*, we work here and are followers of Jesus. We have come to see how you are and to ask if you would like us to pray and ask God to heal your body. Would you like us to do that?'

A look of mild confusion settled on the old man's face as he looked to his son as if to say, 'Did they just ask if they could pray for me? What should I answer . . . ?'

The son looked at his father and then back at us and shrugged his shoulders, 'Of course, please pray for my *Baaba*. We believe that it is only God who can heal us anyway!'

Then everyone relaxed and agreed heartily, 'Yes, yes, only God can heal us! Let's ask him to come and touch your *Baaba* right now.'

Everyone sat up a bit straighter and lifted their palms upwards in submission to God, all eyes fixed on us. I glanced over to the chaplain who had accompanied me as we decided non-verbally which one of us would pray. He wanted to, choosing to pray in Fulfulde as he could tell that this was a Fulbe family. He quietly asked, '*Baaba*, what is your name, please?'

He responded with a glimpse of bemusement, 'Alhadji Hamadou.'

Then the chaplain announced, 'Let's pray then', and he began. The old man and his family all stared as he lifted a prayer of praise to Almighty God in their language and asked him to heal Alhadji Hamadou, to show him how much he loves him, to bless his family and to provide for their needs. 'In the powerful name of Jesus Christ we pray, Amen!'

Then all lifted their palms to their faces as a symbolic act of agreeing and receiving the prayer and joined in with a hearty *Aamina*. Handshakes were exchanged, along with smiles and expressions of thanks. It was a warm moment of connection with this family even though, on this occasion, it did not lead to any deeper conversation. We bade them good evening and moved on to the next patient.

For these Fulbe Muslims it could have been the very first time that they had accepted the prayer of a non-Muslim and a follower of Jesus Christ. It may have been the first time they even realized that Christians pray; Muslims are used to seeing their own people praying in public, but when would they ever see a Christian actually praying? They often have no idea about Christian prayer.

One evening during the prayer round on the children's ward, Lesley from the UK was going from bed to bed with her prayer partner and came across a very sick child in a coma, probably due to malaria. Lesley's instinct was to get down on her knees at the child's bedside and lift her hands to God to ask him to have mercy on this child and heal him. The family could hardly believe what they were seeing; this mature foreign lady was humbling herself and getting on her knees on this dusty floor to pray for their child. In their minds it was only Muslims who got on their knees to pray anyway, so what on earth was going on here? Surely this English lady was not a Muslim, or was she? Her prayer partner joined her there on the floor and everyone else around lifted their palms up to pray for this child. It was a very touching moment and some saw the heart of Christian prayer for the first time; coming to our Father who loves us and hears us, but coming with humility.

This act of simply offering to pray for a sick person has often led to many deeper conversations and opened the door for questions of faith to be asked. The prayer round would act as a filter for us to know who was searching to know more about the gospel and Jesus. One time a man from the Arab Shuwa community was so touched by the prayer for healing that the next day he attributed his marked physical improvement to the power of Jesus and wanted to know how this could be. He had never heard the gospel before but listened intently and accepted a gift of the Gospel of Matthew in his language. The next day he went home, the hospital chaplains assuming they would never see him again. However, a year later this man was back in Meskine, and he came to visit the chaplains in their office. 'Do you remember me? I'm the man you prayed for who got better!' Frankly, the chaplains couldn't quite place him and needed some more information, but after more discussion, they finally remembered him. It turned out that this man was a teacher of the Qur'an to thirteen students, so when he got home he started to teach his students from his Matthew's Gospel because he was so struck by the power and words of Jesus. Never underestimate the power of praying for someone! This man was not only healed and heard the gospel because of it; at least thirteen other people got to hear about Jesus too.

The act of praying for someone in time of need is often an intimate way of showing love and empathy, an opportunity to stand with them in recognition that in our helplessness as human beings there is still the One who can and does draw near to comfort and heal. There have been very tender times during these prayer rounds when we very much sense the presence of God and know that he is making his presence known to the one who is unwell and to those gathered around the bed. Sometimes there have been tears, often there have been smiles. Some people have expressed surprise as we pray to Father God in words that they can understand, as many Muslims are only used to hearing prayers in Arabic, the language of the Qur'an, which they do not understand. When they hear us addressing God with clarity and hope, their hearts are touched and prompted to want to know more about how we can address God in such a way. When others hear us praying in the name of Jesus, it causes them to think more about this man who they have been told is 'just a prophet' and not the Saviour, according to their traditions. The act of praying is more than asking for God's intervention; it is also a way of drawing others into his presence with you, and in so doing, inviting them to know God the Father, Son and Holy Spirit for themselves.

As relationships and conversations evolved out of the prayer rounds, it became our habit to offer the *Jesus* film to people to watch. This film, based on Luke's Gospel, follows the narrative of Jesus' birth and three years of ministry to his ascension. It is the most translated film in the world to date, and we have been blessed in Cameroon to have it available in most languages of the northern people groups. One evening each week the film was projected onto an outside wall in the hospital compound, proving to be very popular, whether it was in Fulfulde or Chadian Arabic. The only problem with this method was that many of the patients themselves could not get outside to see it, so we started to collect portable DVD players that could be distributed to them at the bedside. This became very popular, and so the routine after the prayer round was to then decide who were the priority patients that would see the film that evening and who would have to wait until the next day. If we had kept statistics of how many people have seen the *Jesus* film at Meskine

Hospital in one form or another, then I am sure the numbers would be in the thousands. What a wonderful tool it has been.

Sometimes a visit during the prayer round has provoked a deeper spiritual encounter. Scott experienced this one evening when he visited a Fulbe lady of about 30 years of age named Aissatou. She was typically slim with brightly coloured clothes and had the facial markings of her clan, revealing that she came from the bush. She had travelled from deep in the wilderness of western Chad, along with her husband and family. They came from the nomadic way of life and followed a more syncretistic form of Islam where the use of amulets and charms was commonplace. She had come to the hospital with a chronic health problem, so Scott and his prayer partner offered to pray for her, which she readily accepted. They then moved on to the rest of the patients on the ward. After the prayer round they went back to a neighbouring patient of Aissatou's who had requested a DVD player to watch the *Jesus* film. She was also Fulbe, so was watching the film in Fulfulde that both she and Aissatou could understand. Aissatou, however, became very uncomfortable and distracted when the film started playing but did not stop her neighbour from seeing it. Scott and his partner left, with a plan to come back and visit the lady who had requested the film to see what she had understood.

The next day they went back to the ward to see how the film had been received. Although their intention was to spend time with the lady who had originally asked to watch the *Jesus* film, they were more surprised by the reaction of her neighbour. It seemed that Aissatou had been unable to sleep all night because of the film and was terrified about what had happened. Scott asked her to explain what had frightened her so much and she replied, 'My *ginnaaji* have been very upset by that film about Jesus and haven't allowed me to sleep all night!'

Scott asked her to clarify, 'Are you telling me that you have demons?'

She replied in a very matter-of-fact manner, 'Yes, I've had them since I was a child and they stopped me from sleeping last night.' Then she removed her head covering to reveal two or three little leather amulet pouches that were sewn into her hair. She explained that her *marabout* (traditional healer) had instructed her to wear them in order to keep her demons happy and this had been her habit for many years. Aissatou was bound to wear these amulets for the rest of her life in fear that, if she removed them, the demons would attack her more severely.

Scott went on to ask her if she had watched the *Jesus* film with her neighbour and seen how Jesus had the power over demons, and was able to cast them out of people and heal them. She replied that she had indeed seen that. Scott then offered to explain more about that to her and she was keen to learn, so he accompanied her, along with her sister, to visit the chaplain in his office. Together they began to share the gospel with these ladies, the good news that Jesus came to save us from sin and bring the kingdom of God into our lives, bringing freedom in every way. They explained that in embracing Jesus we become free from the power of Satan and his demons because Jesus has power over every kind of evil. After quite a while of discussion and explanation, Aissatou understood the gospel and with the mustard-seed-sized faith that she had, she prayed to receive Christ as her Lord and as the king of the kingdom of God.

The next step for Aissatou was a huge one. Scott and the chaplain asked Aissatou if she was ready to remove the amulets, as she no longer needed them to control the demons that were troubling her; Jesus was all she needed to protect her now. Aissatou agreed and began to remove the amulets one by one from her hair as they sat there together. She handed them over and asked the men to dispose of them in the best way they saw fit. They suggested that the amulets should be burned and destroyed. Aissatou agreed to this wholeheartedly and so off they went to burn these little amulets that had kept her bound in fear to Satan for so long. Finally, Aissatou was free from the fear that had plagued her since her childhood. The next day she left the hospital and made her way back to the bush of western Chad, with a new story to tell her people about Jesus who has power over Satan and all of their *ginnaajis*.

One of the frustrating things of the hospital ministry is that it is often difficult to follow up people like Aissatou once they leave the hospital because they come to us from such a wide geographical area. The prayer round would often lead us into quite deep conversations with people, and they would open their hearts and minds to the things of Jesus, but then they would go home and the trail of communication would run dry. Sometimes it feels as though you are leaving your new babies to fend for themselves, as they hardly know enough to grow in their new faith and experience of Jesus. They may be illiterate, so giving a Bible will not help; they may not have a phone, so giving a memory card with an audible Bible will not work; they may not want anyone else to know that they have chosen to follow Jesus, as it could put their life in danger. Discipleship of these new believers is difficult.

Lee recalls saying goodbye to a young woman from Chad who had received Christ during her hospital stay. Communication between them had not been easy, as the lady spoke little Fulfulde and Lee did not speak Chadian Arabic, but somehow this lady had understood some of the good news about Jesus. As she got into the bus outside the hospital gates, she looked back at Lee and smiling she said to Lee, '*Iisa, Iisa!*' 'Jesus, Jesus!' That was enough for now, and Lee had to entrust her into the hands of Father God to take care of his new child.

Occasionally though, we get to see the ones we have prayed for and led to Jesus again. Mairamou was one such lady. Mairamou was from the Mousgoum community, mostly found to the east of Meskine, around the waterside towns of Pouss and Maga. Fishing is a way of life for these people. They are often the tallest people in a crowd and fiercely proud of their Mousgoum identity. What makes the Mousgoum people so interesting in comparison to the Fulbe is that it is not their choice of religion that gives them their identity, but purely their language and culture. It is not known exactly, but it seems that there is just about a fifty-fifty split between the Mousgoum Christians and the Mousgoum Muslims, and often the split goes right through the middle of families. What can differentiate them, though, is the way that the women dress. If you are a Mousgoum woman who is a Muslim, you will often be dressed from head to toe in dark, usually black, clothing, with even your face completely covered when in public. This has become their tradition, and that is how Mairamou was dressed when she came to Meskine.

She had come to us with a back problem and was hospitalized for a few days. Her stay coincided with the prayer round, and she was visited by Dr Charis, a general practitioner from the UK, and an occupational therapist from Germany. After they had prayed for her, they continued to chat with Mairamou and explained the gospel to her. She wanted to know more and was keen to watch the *Jesus* film in her language. She was so touched and impressed by what she learned about Jesus that Charis was able to pray with her to receive Jesus as her Lord and Saviour before she went home to her village. Charis never saw her again, but a couple of years later Mairamou came back to Meskine and told her story to the chaplains.

Mairamou explained to them that after she had gone home, full of joy because of what she had discovered about Jesus, she told her husband what had happened, thinking that he too would want to know more. He, however, was not at all happy and became very angry with his wife for becoming a follower of Jesus. He forced her to leave him and their three children for a time, but later allowed her to return home with conditions; she could stay as long as she didn't tell anyone else that she wanted to follow Jesus. If she did, then there would be more trouble for her and she would never see her children again. For the sake of being able to stay with her children, Mairamou agreed to keep her faith to herself.

But Mairamou was desperate to learn more about the man she now called her Lord. She knew that if she brought a Bible into her home, then this would be enough to provoke her husband's anger again. Going to church was also out of the question. But Mairamou had another idea: on Sundays she got into the habit of going near to a church and sitting outside at a distance under the trees. When the service came to an end, she would go up to one or two people coming out and ask them to tell her what they had learned from the sermon and they would explain it to her. She gradually got to know some of the Mousgoum Christians as they befriended her, even expecting her to be waiting for them outside church each Sunday. After some time, it became evident to her new friends that she had truly accepted Christ, so the evangelist from the church took her way out into the bush to a stream and baptized her. He also taught her some prayers that she could say when she was at home on her own and some Bible verses that she could hold in her heart. To this day, Mairamou prays these prayers and feeds on the Bible verses that she has memorized.

God has also made another special way to encourage Mairamou in her faith. She says that she regularly hears Jesus talking to her and sees him in her dreams. When asked how she knew it was Jesus speaking to her, this was her reply: 'I see a man who is shining brightly, but I can't see the features of his face. Whenever he talks to me, it brings me a feeling of peace and courage; he tells me not to be afraid and to keep believing in the way of following him. Sometimes Satan tries to speak to me too, but I know the difference between Jesus and Satan; Satan never brings peace or love. He only tries to make me afraid, but Jesus never makes me afraid, only strong.'

Mairamou still wears the heavy, dark clothes that she is forced to wear by the community she belongs to. She says that she hates to wear them and longs to throw them away but feels she must continue in order to honour her husband. Since Mairamou has started following Jesus, though, she now sees the clothing as a physical reminder to her every day that Jesus is with her. The truth is, God has taught her what it means to be 'clothed with Christ'.[2]

As the prayer round became an established part of the identity of Meskine Hospital, we have also endeavoured to enable every person who wants to know more about Jesus be able to do just that when they are with us. We would even see it as failing in what we had come to Cameroon to do if someone had left us without being offered a taste of Jesus. As surgery had become such a major part of the work, it was not surprising that many of the surgical patients had the opportunity to learn about Jesus too. Some of them were unforgettable to us.

6

When Only an Operation Will Do

Raymond, the Elephant Man

It's not every day that a man arrives at Meskine Hospital carrying his intestines in his hands, so when Raymond did just that it was unforgettable. Raymond, being an expert in elephants, was working with the WWF[1] as part of their elephant surveillance team in Cameroon, and the project had taken him to Waza National Park, about an hour and a half's drive from Meskine. It is one of the few tourist attractions in the region and, in safer days past, was a regular destination for our team and visitors to get a taste of the beauty of the Sahel landscape and the wildlife found there. On a good day it was possible to see large groups of elephants munching their way through the dusty, dried-out grass, or quenching their thirst at the shrinking water holes. The sound of many elephants eating a meal can be astonishingly loud as grass roots are pulled up and chomped, tree branches are grabbed, and heavy legs wander over the hard earth.

The WWF's task at this time was to put tracker collars on the elephants so they could be better looked after. Poachers were, and still are, a constant menace, so much so that these days the elephant population in Cameroon is much reduced. In order to attach the collars on the elephants, a tranquillizing drug is given to put the elephant to sleep. When the job is done, a reversal drug is given to wake the elephant up again. Normally, this gives the team enough time to get out of the way before the elephant wakes up. On this day, however, one elephant woke up much quicker than expected and Raymond was still too close. As the elephant moved and swung his head, he was gored in the abdomen and all around one side, extending to his back, by the elephant's tusk. In a flurry of shock, panic and pain he tried to get some distance between himself and the elephant as the rest of his team ran to help him and get out of the elephant's way. This had become a very serious situation very quickly. They were out in the middle of nowhere and a man's intestines were leaking out of him.

At this time Dr John Baigent[2] was the medical director at Meskine. On the night of Raymond's injury, the surgical team received a phone call from the WWF team to say they were on their way with their wounded colleague and would be there as soon as they could. Dr John was called by the surgical team leader for that night and wandered over to the hospital, wondering what he was about to find. As Raymond was brought into the emergency room the large, gaping hole in his side was obvious, and he had already lost a lot of blood. Raymond was quickly wheeled to the operating room where Dr John and his team explored the hole. The mud and grass from Waza National Park was still in the gore-wound, which was so large that they could see Raymond's kidney. This was not going to be easy. They carefully cleared out all the muck, and checked the tissues and delicate structures to see what had been perforated by the elephant's tusk, followed by the methodical process of sewing it all back together again.

Then began the 'watch and wait' job that comes after any surgery, to see if all was well. Had everything been repaired?

Was there any infection? Was Raymond going to regain his strength quickly enough? What followed was a huge relief to all. It soon became apparent that things were going very well with no complications, so it was decided that Raymond could be transferred to a hospital in Yaounde, where he lived with his family. Being with WWF, it was possible for a private plane to be arranged to transport him from the local airport to the capital city in the south. Raymond was still weak, but so pleased with the care he had received at Meskine that he asked Dr John to accompany him on the journey to Yaounde. Dr John was happy to oblige, considering the severity of this man's injuries.

Dr John was welcomed into Raymond's family home in Yaounde, while Raymond himself was taken straight to a hospital for ongoing care. For the next few days John was warmly invited by the family to share about Jesus and pray for them, even having the privilege of praying with one of Raymond's daughters to commit her life to Jesus. It was thrilling for John to have this exceptional time with the family of a man he had operated on. It was obvious that God had turned this crisis into a blessing for Raymond and his family and, happily, Raymond made a full recovery from his injuries. We do not know, however, if he continued to work with elephants . . .

Right from the inception of Meskine Hospital, the noble, hard work of surgery was bound to be a central part of its identity, as MCWA's founder was Dr Bert Oubre, an exceptionally good general surgeon and teacher of surgery. It was his vision to provide a good-quality medical service to the far north province of Cameroon that led to Meskine Hospital coming into existence, and it was not long before it became known as a place where you could trust the surgical team to do a very good job. Being able to offer this surgical service has meant that Meskine Hospital was always more than a basic health centre and became a place to refer patients from all over the region. If surgery was required, then the first choice for most people in the area was Meskine. The *suudu seekugo*, or 'cutting room', also called 'Bloc', became a place where lives were saved, of miracles, and of the origin of many relationships.

One of the challenges facing the MCWA team when they were setting up the hospital was finding the calibre of employees who could be trained to a high standard of medical expertise. For Dr Oubre this meant taking people who had never entered a surgical room and teaching them from the very basics to the very complicated, so they in turn could carry out the surgical procedures themselves. Alongside all the practical training that Bert gave them, he also modelled and instilled in his team an essential part of every surgical procedure: the absolute necessity to pray for and over each patient before they made the first cut, asking God to guide their hands, to give them wisdom and for Jesus our Healer to come and do his wonderful life-giving work. Bert impressed the importance of this habit on his students to the extent that they would see it as being as important as scrubbing their hands clean before every operation. To this day no procedure is carried out in Bloc until God has been invited to come and take control.

Dr Carsten, the Surgeon

In addition to Bert Oubre's training, it has been MCWA's privilege to welcome many visiting surgeons over the years, their visits ranging from a few days to a few years. Carsten Kretzschmar is just one of this vast team building upon Bert Oubre's legacy and contributing to the training and encouragement of the resident surgical team. Dr Carsten, from Germany, came with his wife and three children for over three years in 2009. As is the case with all families who come to Meskine for a significant amount of time, their 'Meskine home' became an established part of their family history forever, and their experiences there have left an indelible mark on their lives.

Carsten loves being a surgeon and had dreamed of being one since childhood. The ultimate fulfilment of his purpose and calling was being able to practise his dream job in Africa. In comparison to being a surgeon in Germany, Carsten loved the simplicity of the job in Meskine, without the layers of bureaucracy. The vibrant team collaboration in Bloc and on the wards with the Cameroonian staff, and the very relational interaction with his patients more than made up for the lack of technical developments and equipment. He learned to depend completely on God when challenging situations were before him – which turned out to be quite frequently, as you never knew what the next patient would present you with.

Carsten discovered a major challenge in the large numbers of children coming with serious complications from typhoid, mainly perforations of the small intestine which were notoriously difficult to suture and repair. One boy, whose abdomen Carsten had already operated on several times, was not healing and they were running out of options, but in God's perfect timing he brought a specialist from the USA to Meskine for a few weeks just when Carsten needed some new ideas from a more experienced surgeon to help this boy. They decided to create an ileostomy, bypassing the worn-out small intestines altogether. However, due to the already advanced inflammation, the wound was just not healing; Carsten had almost given up hope that this boy could heal. The only way possible was through the risky technique of open treatment of the wounds and not suturing them at all. After much prayer and patience, the boy did become well again and the surgical team celebrated it as another miracle.

It was not unusual for Carsten to bring his complicated cases up at our missionary team gatherings, asking for prayer especially when a difficult surgical case like this boy was coming up. When we met as a team again the following week, it was always encouraging to hear that the surgery had gone according to plan. A happy ending wasn't guaranteed though, and Carsten had to face the reality of not having intensive care facilities at Meskine. Knowing that if that same patient had been in Germany they might have survived is a hard thing to come to terms with, but Carsten appreciated the opportunities that came with helping people to die with dignity and compassion. Good medical care is not all about the latest technology and techniques, but also about respecting the one who is looking to you for help and doing what you can with love.

Operations on children became a regular thing for Carsten, especially in cases of osteomyelitis, where bones become deeply infected and often take months to heal. These children end up being away from home and school for so long that they become isolated from their social situations as their world shrinks to the walls of the children's ward and the mat on the ground outside. Carsten's wife, Annett, was so struck by this that she initiated gathering these 'long-term children' together on the ward to do simple schoolwork, hear Bible stories and play together while they waited for the healing of their bodies – a gesture of love that was hugely appreciated by these children and their families. Like these children, so many of the surgical patients who have passed through Meskine have experienced so much more than just the healing of their bodies, as the following few stories show.

Hawa, the Business Woman

After twenty years of MCWA's presence in Meskine, following much discussion and prayer, Dave, Patsy[3] and I moved to the nearby town of Maroua to extend our outreach to the Fulbe community. In 2013 we found ourselves setting up our new home in what felt like a world away, but was in fact only 5 miles from Meskine. As part of the process of figuring out where to go prior to this move, we had ventured to another town in the area that was a predominantly Muslim community. We wondered if this would be a good place to relocate, as historically there hadn't been much outreach with the gospel there. We went on a research visit for a few days, but the problem was we didn't know anyone, and there was no hotel or guest-house to stay in. During the first day we met Sarki, who worked for the *lamiido*[4] of the town and was in charge of the butchering and selling of meat. Sarki was a tall, dark man with a loud voice and broad smile and, surprisingly, the hint of cigarette smoke lingering on his flowing robes.

Sarki understood our predicament of not having anywhere to stay, and his hospitality came bubbling out of him. 'You must come and stay with me, all of you. I have plenty of room and I'm not afraid of white people. I won't hear of you going anywhere else. Come to my house. God has brought us together!' And that was the decision made. We followed Sarki to his home, a compound full of scattered buildings and little alleyways. Having three wives and many children it was not a quiet place, but we gratefully accepted his invitation for three days. Food was in plentiful supply, and since Sarki was in charge of meat for the whole town, it was no surprise to be given more than enough of it at every meal.

Dr Jacqueline[5] also accompanied us on this trip, and it wasn't long before people heard that she was in town. A doctor from Meskine Hospital in the neighbourhood was too good an opportunity to miss. Jacqueline patiently listened to their ailments as they came by to see her. Among them was Hawa, Sarki's sister, who just happened to be visiting her brother for a few days.

Hawa was a beautiful woman to look at, and with her bright eyes and her warm manner, it was a pleasure to have a conversation with her. It turned out that Hawa was quite the business woman and often travelled the length of Cameroon taking care of her affairs in the south. Her success meant that she had the means to go to Mecca on pilgrimage, which added to her status in society. It was very clear that Hawa was much loved and admired by her brother's family and it was with concern that Sarki brought her to see the doctor.

On examining her, it was obvious to Jacqueline that Hawa had a suspicious lump that needed to be seen right away at the hospital. Hawa stated that she had taken antibiotics several times but it hadn't got any better so wasn't sure if going to a hospital again would do any good. Jacqueline gently but firmly explained that it was likely that she needed surgery now to remove the lump as it could be cancer, but only a biopsy would prove this. She implored her to come as soon as possible, as waiting would only make things worse. Hawa agreed that she would indeed come to Meskine very soon and they exchanged phone numbers.

Frustratingly for Dr Jacqueline and sadly for Hawa, she did not come until eight months later. Hawa had some pressing business that she wanted to finish before she had her operation, but it had taken so much longer than she thought it would.

Then there were family issues and events going on, and what with one thing and another the eight months slipped by so fast. By the time she came to Meskine to see Jacqueline and the surgical team her cancer had become much more advanced – worryingly so. The team in Bloc did radical surgery and removed the lymph glands that had also become involved, hoping that it would be enough but knowing that it could all have been done too late. If only Hawa had come earlier. This is the scenario too often repeated. The understanding of modern medicine and surgery by many in northern Cameroon is limited, the general thought being that if nothing else works then going to hospital is the last option, rather than seeing it as the first option.

Hawa's recovery from this major surgery actually went very well and she stayed for two weeks until her extensive wound had healed up. Her financial means enabled her to complete two rounds of expensive chemotherapy too, and she thought she had done enough to beat the cancer – surely it would all be enough to cure her? Some members of her family thought she had even gone too far by accepting this surgery; surely it was being overcautious and unnecessary. But six months later it was clear that it had been too little, too late, and the tumours aggressively returned. Hawa's heart was broken. She was in increasing pain and not sleeping well. This time she knew she was dying.

Patsy and I had continued to visit Hawa at her home after her surgery as it was not far from our new home. We got to know her mother and other siblings over these months but had not been able to talk to them about deeper things of faith and Jesus; the door to share good news did not appear to be open to us. With the recurrence of the cancer we had an increased sense of urgency, as we could see that Hawa might only be with us for a few more weeks. The tension in our hearts was heavy; on the one hand we knew we had to tell her the good news about Jesus, but on the other hand we couldn't bear the rejection of Jesus that we had so often heard. The sad dismissal to hearing the gospel that we had become so used to hearing – 'But Jesus didn't die on the cross, so how can he be the Saviour?' – was still echoing in our ears from when we had tried to talk to Hawa's sister recently. We earnestly prayed for an open door to talk to Hawa about Jesus before it was too late.

Finally, the day came. Hawa was looking thinner and paler but still sitting up and chatting. Her sister was at her side as always, lovingly taking care of her; their mother was outside, resting on a mat in the shade. It was a quiet moment and we seized it. Both Patsy and I sensed the presence of the Holy Spirit with us as we gently and quietly shared the good news about Jesus with them – about the assurance he gives us, the freedom from the fear of dying that knowing Jesus brings. I was able to share my own experience of peace when I had been so ill and thought I was dying ten years previously in 2004, with the sudden onset of paralysis caused by a virus. They were listening attentively, asking questions, nodding their heads and clicking their tongues in agreement from time to time. We discussed together how Jesus was spoken of in the Qur'an and how he differed in every way from all the other prophets.

As our conversation proceeded, Hawa shared with us that she had recently had a dream. She described seeing a dark man who came near to her but she knew he would not bring her peace, only fear; then she saw a bright, shining man who came and sat with her and he did bring her peace. She wondered who these men were. It has been our experience over the years that many Muslims are having dreams in which they meet a man like this who is bright and shining. Often they can't see his facial features, but his presence and words bring comfort, peace, strength and life; the conclusion of most is that this is Jesus Christ. We could not tell Hawa that she had met Jesus in her dream for sure, but we did explain that this is the experience of many others. We had to leave the work of conviction to the Holy Spirit, but we were thankful that we had been given the opportunity to speak clearly of Jesus and the way of salvation. As we left Hawa's home that day, Patsy and I were full of relief and thanksgiving.

As far as we know Hawa did not say 'yes' to Jesus that day. The next time we saw her after this conversation she was too weak to sit up, too tired and in too much pain to have a long conversation. We had to leave her in the hands of Father God, trusting that he knows those who are his. We were thankful, though, to have had that special moment with Hawa and her family at just the right time when she was still able to hear the gospel. She died a few weeks after that. It is our hope that we will see her again one day and that meeting Jesus in her dreams brought her safely home.

Yaya, the Shepherd

The life of people in the most rural parts of northern Cameroon is often a matter of routine and therefore fairly predictable, but being so far from the larger communities and authorities means there are incidents of opportunistic robberies on the roads, out in the bush and in the villages. These attacks can often turn violent, leaving the victims injured if they manage to escape with their lives. One day when Yaya was out in the bush, he found himself confronted by a group of men set on stealing whatever money he had on him. When they couldn't find any after making Yaya turn out all his pockets, they were so angry that they shot him in the chest with a bow and arrow, and fled. Somehow, Yaya managed to get back to his people, and they immediately took him to a hospital in the nearest town, where he stayed for two weeks. All this time the metal, barbed arrow-head, which was the size of an ink pen, was still stuck in Yaya's chest. For reasons that were never explained, the medical staff at that hospital did not deal with the problem and Yaya was gradually getting weaker and more unwell. Finally, the family decided to look for help elsewhere and brought him to Meskine.

The problem was obvious: the arrow-head had to be removed immediately. The surgical team got to work as soon as possible on the day that Yaya arrived. In the end, the surgery to remove the offending object was not that complicated, but it was vital. As it had been there for so long, Yaya's lungs were not functioning well and he had a serious infection requiring him to stay at the hospital for an extended time. Scott and the chaplains met Yaya one evening during the prayer round not long after his surgery, and were welcomed warmly by Yaya to pray for his healing. Scott returned later to offer Yaya the *Jesus* film in Fulfulde to watch and, again, he received it very warmly and ended up watching it several times. Just a couple of days later, after discussing what he had been learning about Jesus with the chaplains, Yaya announced that he was very ready to ask Jesus to come into his life, as he wanted to follow him too; it seems that God had prepared this man to recognize his need of Jesus. Gradually, Yaya made an excellent recovery from his wounds and happily returned to his village. He and his family were extremely thankful and grateful for the care he had received, knowing that the surgery had saved Yaya's life. Yaya also knew that he had experienced another salvation when he met Jesus and cherished this in his heart as he went home.

Sometime later, Yaya returned to Meskine to visit the chaplains and Scott. They were overjoyed to see him looking so well, having obviously regained his health. They took advantage of having some uninterrupted time with him alone, to chat and encourage him in his new life with Jesus. At this time Yaya had not told his family of his decision to follow Jesus and had had no other contact with Christians, so this visit was like fanning the embers of his faith to keep the fire burning. When they parted ways again, the chaplains gave Yaya a small, solar-charged MP3 player that he could use at home to listen to Bible stories, in order to help him grow more in his understanding of the gospel.

Months later, having heard nothing from Yaya, Scott and one of the hospital chaplains decided to go and find him in his village. Yaya didn't have a phone, so they couldn't tell him they were on their way. When they arrived in his remote village it was more than a surprise, a shock even, when their car approached.

Yaya and his people were Fulbe from the nomadic tradition. For generations they had followed a pastoral route with their cattle between Cameroon and Nigeria, but in recent years they had become more settled and started farming, alongside keeping their cattle. For them this was a huge change of lifestyle, and in some ways it made them feel as if they were living nearer to the rest of the world. The location of their village, however, was still far out into the bush, found at the end of a dusty, narrow track. The fact that the visitors were able to find them was a major achievement that day.

Yaya welcomed his friends to his simple home built from mud with a grass roof, and they sat down in the shade to exchange greetings with lots of handshakes and smiles. After a while of chatting together, Yaya began to express some of the difficulties he had experienced with his people since returning from his visit to Meskine. He had started listening to the Bible stories on the MP3-player with his family, but sadly they had not received it as good news at all. In fact, they had become very angry, the older men of the community telling him to stop listening to it immediately and threatening him with more trouble if he refused. This strong reaction upset and intimidated Yaya, causing him to lose all courage and hope of ever talking about Jesus with them again. The visitors listened to their friend's words with heavy hearts, as this was not an uncommon reaction for many Fulbe who have come to Christ; what is received as good news by one member of the family is then rejected as bad news by the rest.

Scott and the chaplain were invited to stay that night with Yaya and his family, which they were more than happy to do. Fulbe hospitality to guests is unparalleled in its generosity and the visitors' needs were well taken care of. Some of Yaya's family knew he had seen the *Jesus* film when he was at Meskine Hospital, so when Scott offered to show it to the whole neighbourhood on a makeshift screen that evening, they accepted, curiosity getting the better of them. In reality, though, they were not enthusiastic and remained rather aloof from the visitors during the rest of their stay. After the visit, Scott learned that the neighbours were actually afraid of him, as they had never had a white man come to visit them before. Their instinctive reaction was that something must be wrong for this foreigner to come out into the bush and look for them specifically. Was he sent by the government? Was he looking to find fault with them in some way? Had Yaya done something wrong that they came especially to see him? The fact that it was completely the opposite and was simply a visit among friends was sadly misunderstood. It was another lesson for visitors to Cameroon that

our foreignness and white skin can so often get in the way of
what we intend.

Not long after this visit, terrorists began to launch attacks in
Cameroon in the region where Yaya was situated; consequently,
it was no longer wise to venture out there to see him and keeping in touch was very difficult. We do not know if Yaya was
ever able to share the good news of Jesus with his family again,
but we do know that he himself received it wholeheartedly and
clung to it despite the opposition around him.

Pierre, the Soldier

In 2001, when Dr Jim from the USA was working with us,
there was an astonishing arrival at the hospital one day. All of
a sudden, there were several military vehicles and armed soldiers bustling around the entrance and they were definitely in a
hurry. One of their men was seriously injured and needed help
immediately. The details of the situation were not clear, but
whatever had happened had disturbed the rest of his company.

The injured soldier was transferred onto a trolley and
wheeled to the operating room for Dr Jim and the team to
assess. Now, Dr Jim was an experienced surgeon from New
York City and had been exposed to a lot of different scenarios,
but what he saw that day was a completely new experience for
him. The soldier's name was Pierre. He was covered in blood
and it was obvious where it had all come from. From his mouth
all the way up to his forehead was one gigantic hole, making
his features completely unrecognizable. The man's eyes were
not even visible, such was the extent of the mess. It was obvious that he had been shot in the face, the bullet leaving a huge
trench right through the middle.

As the facts emerged, it turned out that Pierre had not been shot in battle, nor by mistake; rather he had been involved in an altercation with his commanding officer and had become extremely angry. In a fit of rage, he had shot and killed the officer with a rifle and then turned it on himself in an effort to commit suicide by placing the barrel of the rifle under his chin. His hope was to blow his own brains out, but the line of fire was not aimed in that direction, it was too far forward, so Pierre only managed to blow his face apart, missing his brain completely. The bullet went from under the jaw, through the mouth and exited through his forehead!

Incredibly, Dr Jim and the surgical team were able to save Pierre's life that day, but it took several more surgical procedures in the following days to sew his face back together again. It was very challenging for everyone involved and nothing like anything any of them had done before. In the more developed medical world, facial reconstruction is a highly specialized area of surgery, but the team had to get on and do whatever they could to give Pierre some kind of functional face again so that he could eat and talk. Amazingly, Pierre had not lost any of his senses in the shooting; he could still see, smell, hear and taste. For several weeks he had heavy bandages wrapped around his head, but gradually the wounds began to heal, the bandages were reduced and Pierre began to talk and eat again.

Throughout his stay at Meskine, Pierre was kept under armed guard and never left alone, as he was officially under arrest for killing his commanding officer, but the chaplains were allowed to visit him and gradually got to know him. It wasn't long before they offered Pierre a portable cassette player so that he could listen to teaching from the Bible while he recovered. Pierre was not a Christian at that time but gladly received it and could often be found with his headphones on, listening to the tapes. We do not know if he ever welcomed Jesus into his life, nor do we know what happened to Pierre when he left the hospital. It was certain that he would have been sentenced for what he had done, and it was very probable that he was executed, such was the seriousness of his crime. What we do know is that Pierre was given an extension to his life, and we trust that God was able to draw near to him during those days while he was with us, in order to prepare him for what was waiting for him when he left.

As much as possible the medical team at Meskine Hospital has strived to help each patient that has been presented to them, even in challenging situations like Pierre's, but at times there have been complicated cases that have come through the door that require resources way beyond the scope of a little facility on the edge of a desert.

7

Can Anyone Else Help Us?

Jacques

Papa was having an average kind of day for a farmer in his village in rural Chad, battling with the sun and the soil in order to feed his family. His 10-year-old son, Jacques, was enjoying his average day climbing up into the trees to pick mangoes, something that he and his friends had become rather good at. The big, swollen fruit full of sweet, sticky juice dared them to reach just a little bit further along the branch. But this day would turn into catastrophe when Jacques lost his balance as he reached out and fell downwards, landing astride onto a lower branch. The pain he felt was instant and the damage to his urethra would dictate the events of his and his father's lives for the next months. There would be no more average days for a long time.

Because of the damage done to Jacques' urethra, it became extremely difficult for him to urinate as there was no longer a free-flowing way out from his bladder. Jacques had to squat down and use so much abdominal pressure trying to urinate that his bowels also became prolapsed. This became a daily nightmare for him. Papa took his son to various hospitals in Chad to try to get the problem resolved, but after several unsuccessful surgeries to dilate the urethra he was becoming despondent, so on hearing about Meskine he decided to make the long journey for one more try; maybe this hospital in Cameroon could help his son.

When Jacques was examined by Dr John and the surgical team they decided to have one more go at the dilatation surgery as that was their only option. As with every other procedure, they prayed for God's help and guidance beforehand, especially knowing that this was not going to be an easy case. Indeed, it turned out to be impossible, as they could hardly get the dilator inserted at all. As John was trying to find a way, he sensed God putting a thought in his mind: if he could get Jacques to England, he knew a solution could be found. But how could this be achieved? The funding and the logistics of getting this rural boy from Chad to England seemed beyond reach. Thinking and praying about the situation, John contacted his friend in England who was a genito-urinary surgeon, to discuss Jacques' predicament. His friend's specialist team offered to help and so John and Lesley set to work on how to put this plan in motion.

Things started to move quickly. After just a few weeks of paperwork, phone calls and fundraising, all was organized and they were finally cleared to make the journey, which would start with a flight from the local airport. Papa and his son were a picture of apprehension and excitement as they were driven to the airport with their few possessions. There was still a big problem, though, as their passports hadn't arrived yet. The authorities had announced that the documents would be in the postal sack arriving on the plane they were due to fly out on, and the airport officials would allow the sack to be opened on the runway to retrieve the passports. So right there, outside the plane, the mail sack was opened, but disappointingly no passports were found that day. The unforeseen journey back to

Meskine Hospital was made with solemn faces and in silence, telling of the huge anticlimax for father and son. They had to wait for a little while longer.

Another week went by before the passports finally arrived, and father and son returned to the airport. There were several nuns who happened to be travelling south on the same flight and were delighted to accompany Jacques and his father to make sure they got off the plane at the right place – after all, neither of them spoke any French, so from now on they would be entering a world of confusion. After goodbyes were exchanged, John and Lesley watched Papa and Jacques climb up the steps and into the aircraft. They could only wonder how their friends were feeling as the plane took off. As it got smaller and smaller in the sky, they expressed their thankfulness to God for the successful first part of this massive undertaking.

Papa and Jacques somehow managed to navigate their way through the international airports and arrived in London to be welcomed by a local pastor, and Andy and Rachel Picton who had previously worked at Meskine Hospital. Much to the relief of Papa and Jacques, they were finally with people they could talk to as they had the Fulfulde language in common. For a few days the Pictons helped them adjust to being in the UK.

The visitors later moved to the pastor's home, and preparations and appointments were made with the medical team. The operation and recovery went extremely well, and Jacques was discharged after a week with his urethra finally dilated. The surgeon would not allow Jacques to fly home until he'd had a final check-up four weeks later, so the pastor and his family kindly took care of him and his father for this extended stay. This was part of a huge effort of generosity and kindness that was shown to this family by so many people to cover the costs of the trip: friends of the Baigents, Pictons and several churches, even a complete stranger who knocked at the pastor's door and gave him a significant amount of money to help. The surgeon and anaesthetist did not even charge for their services and expertise. This had indeed been an extraordinary display of love which led to Jacques' healing.

On the last leg of the homeward flight from Douala to Maroua, God again provided an escort for Papa and his son to ensure they arrived at their destination. Dr John was waiting for them at Meskine and anxious to see the results of this marathon journey. The reunion was sweet and the relief was tangible in the air as they greeted, but the doctor was not satisfied until he watched Jacques pass urine. On seeing the result, John triumphantly declared, 'He passes urine like an elephant!' Jacques was healed and God was praised that day. They were now free to return home to their village in Chad with an adventure story to tell. Jacques was able to restart his schooling now that he was free from the debilitating result of his accident, and grew up to become a handsome and confident young man.

Being a remote hospital in the sub-Sahara has its challenges on most days for the medical staff, but more often than not a way can be found to overcome them somehow. The frustration of not having the medications available that would be most beneficial for the patient can usually be eased by finding a decent alternative. The lack of choices when it comes to diagnostic tools makes the doctors feel like banging their heads against the nearest wall at times, but in the end some careful detective work and treating-by-elimination often gets to the root of the problem. At times, though, there are people like Jacques who come through the door of Meskine Hospital who absolutely need help from specialist doctors and surgeons that just can't be found nearby. These are the days when being a general hospital reveals its limitations and the call goes out for help further afield. Over the years MCWA has been privileged to be a part of the care chain that has significantly contributed to the wellbeing of a number of special people.

Abel

The UK-based non-profit organization Willing and Abel[1] was started by the incredible visionary surgeon Dr Abigail Estelle in 2009. We had the pleasure of welcoming her to Meskine Hospital for a short visit in March of that year, which coincided with the birth of Abel. He was safely delivered on our maternity ward, but Abel was born with a severe rare heart defect called ectopia cordis, when the heart is positioned outside of the chest cavity and is completely visible. When a child comes into the world like this, it is a huge shock and almost unbelievable to those who witness it. This tiny new person is being kept alive by the fragile pump that is exposed, completely unprotected and extremely vulnerable. Normally the rib cage provides the natural protection that the heart needs, but for Abel there was nothing between it and the rest of the world. Specialist surgery was required if this little boy was going to survive, but it was not something we were equipped to do in Meskine. Dr Abi was so struck by this little boy's plight that it prompted her into action immediately. After a very short amount of time she had raised funds and organized for Abel to be transferred to San Donato Bambino Cardiac Centre in Milan, Italy. The surgery was successfully carried out to reposition Abel's heart within his chest and repair his diaphragm, and after just a few weeks of recovery, Abel and his mother returned home to Cameroon. She was the happiest mother of a healthy little boy, who now had his heart in the right place.

Socially, however, things were not going so well for Abel and his family at home. His parents were from a farming community and were struggling to make ends meet. Added to the effects of being part of a drinking culture, it was soon evident that ongoing medical care for the children was not a high priority for this family.

Sadly, Abel died of complications from cerebral malaria just two years later, but his name lives on in Willing and Abel. Dr Abi and her team continue to arrange specialist surgical intervention for other children from Cameroon, across Africa and the developing world. The following two stories reflect the ongoing help that Abel's short life instigated with the formation of this special organization.

Aboubakar

Little Aboubakar's life was turned upside down when he was at home one hot day. It was not an unusual day in any way and, as is the custom after playing hard on a hot day, the first thing on your mind is to quench your thirst. For this 5-year-old boy, it was impossible for him to discern that what he was about to drink was not water but another colourless liquid that would burn the inside of his oesophagus as soon as it was swallowed. It was lye water that had been prepared for use in cooking by boiling the ashes from the fire and saving the alkaline liquid. In Cameroon this potent caustic liquid is still used in very small quantities as the western equivalent of baking soda. As he gulped it down Aboubakar instantly knew that this was not the water he was expecting, as a burning, choking sensation rose in his throat. He threw down the bowl and started to cough and gag, trying to get the feeling to stop. His coughing led to vomiting as he struggled to gain control, but the damage was already done. The delicate soft tissues of his insides had been burned by the lye water to such an extent that eating and drinking became so painful for him that he could hardly contemplate even trying. His family took him to the nearest hospital for help, but soon after, they were referred to Meskine Hospital, as it became evident that this was a very serious and challenging situation.

By the time Aboubakar came to us he had become dangerously thin and undernourished, simply because eating was virtually impossible for him. There was such a narrowed oesophagus for the food to pass through that it was very painful for him to eat and he would feel as if he was choking as he fought to swallow it down. Even liquid was difficult and took all his effort. It was necessary to set up a feeding line directly into his stomach in order for him to get any meaningful nutrition to keep him alive. With tender loving care from the team on the children's ward and special attention from Kari, a nurse from the USA, and her husband, Andy, Aboubakar began to regain some of his strength and sparkle, and even began to smile again and have the energy to play a little.

It was a huge relief to hospital staff and family that this little boy had improved so much, but the care he was receiving was only a short-term solution to a very serious long-term problem. Aboubakar needed surgery to stretch and open up his very much narrowed oesophagus again, and we simply could not do that kind of operation in Meskine. It required a specialist surgeon and team to take care of him. In 2010, with the help of Willing and Abel, the right medical facility and team was found at Grey's Hospital, Pietermaritzburg, South Africa, who agreed to carry out the incredible surgical procedure of a gastric pull-up on Aboubakar. He set off on the journey of a lifetime to the other end of the continent with his mother and a friend, who had agreed to go as she could understand a smattering of English, which would be vital to help this family navigate the unknown.

After a couple of months Aboubakar came back home as a fit and healthy boy, with chubby cheeks and more energy than he had had since his ordeal began. He has been able to live a normal, healthy life ever since.

Aissa – Told by Sarah Ford

When I [Sarah][2] first met Aissa in 2009, she was sitting with her aunt by the hospital pharmacy. Her head was wrapped in a dirty rag and she was covered with flies. I could smell infection from about five feet away, telling me that this was a seriously ill little girl. I asked them to follow me into the examination room so that I could have a good look at where the awful smell was coming from.

Upon examination I found that Aissa had a huge sore extending from her eye, which was swollen shut, down to her jaw and the corner of her lips, thus engulfing her whole cheek. She was diagnosed with cancrum oris, an illness which starts with a simple infection, such as an abscessed tooth, but once neglected begins to eat away at the face. This infection had become out of control, and at approximately 6 years old, Aissa only weighed 24 pounds and was dangerously anaemic. The prognosis for Aissa was not looking good.

I discovered that Aissa had been abandoned by her mother, who had left her father to marry someone else. According to the cultural norm, women generally don't enter a new marriage with children from a previous relationship, so Aissa was left with her father, who struggled with alcoholism, and her elderly grandmother. Their home was in a remote village towards the hills. This isolation was mingled with poverty, and these were the main reasons that Aissa's illness became so severe before the family sought intervention.

From our first meeting I felt overwhelming compassion for Aissa and just knew that I had to help her in whatever way I could. However, the general feeling of the medical team was that this little girl was not going to get better, so was it even worth trying? The expense and the effort would probably be for nothing. Initially, Aissa's family declined hospitalization and desired to return to their village, where she would surely have died. In their minds they thought that they would come and get some medication for Aissa and then go home; it had certainly not occurred to them to stay for a long period of time. It would have been completely reasonable to let them go. This skeletal girl had such a poor prognosis, it might have seemed irrational to expect her to heal. However, I sensed that it was the Holy Spirit who had guided me towards her, who prompted me to fight for her. We had to at least try.

After much discussion, the family finally agreed to stay for a few days to see what could be done. Following her hospitalization on the children's ward, Aissa was taken to the surgical Bloc where the infected portions of her face were removed, along with a few teeth. A nasogastric tube was inserted so that she could start getting some nutrition. After a donation from one of the missionaries, Aissa also received a blood transfusion to treat her severe anaemia, and within the week her appetite returned; she was able to sit up, smile and begin to play again. The turnaround was incredible and Aissa began to thrive. This strong-willed and sassy girl soon became a regular fixture at the hospital, the local market and our corner of the village. The emaciated child who had turned up a few months previously had been transformed into a glorious bundle of life and energy.

Once the infection had been cleared and Aissa was out of initial danger, her face began to heal. However, she still had a large hole where her cheek used to be. Reconstruction surgery was essential to restore her face and allow her to live without stigma, but this was not available in Meskine, as it was a complicated procedure. Dr Abi knew the surgical staff of the *Africa Mercy*, one of the hospital ships belonging to the organization Mercy Ships. Their surgical coordinator agreed to repair Aissa's facial deformity if she could get to the ship when it was based in Togo. Willing and Abel organization offered to meet the financial costs for this extensive trip, so we began the long preparations. Paperwork, passports, phone calls and emails became a necessary part of my work for a while.

The time eventually came for Aissa, her father and me to travel to the ship for the corrective facial surgery. This in itself is a huge story, but suffice to say that it was successful and Aissa finally had her cheek back. Thanks to the ongoing help of Bethlehem Foundation, a Catholic centre taking care of vulnerable children near to Meskine, Aissa was able to grow up in an environment of safety and love. Willing and Abel have a wonderful strapline, 'See the one, love the one' and this notion, put into practice through the helping hands of many, was beautifully displayed in Aissa's life.

Emergency Medical Evacuation

Across Africa there have been many emergency medical evacuations of visiting foreigners who can suddenly make use of their medical insurance to get them to a place of better medical care as soon as possible. There can hardly be anything more stark to reveal the different worlds that collide when visitors come to Africa and work alongside locals; the truth is that there are different rules in getting access to good medical care, depending on where you were born. When you become an illustration of this difference yourself, it is rather humbling and troubling, leading to much soul-searching. This became my experience in 2004.

One morning as I cycled to the hospital, I knew I didn't have much energy and attributed it to the fact that I was still recovering from a recent bout of flu. It was also the middle of hot season and everything you did just felt like hard work, sapping your energy, so I told myself to simply get on with the job. As the morning dragged on, I developed a deep ache in my back and felt extremely tired, so I asked my physiotherapy colleague to continue without me and cycled home again. I thought I just needed lots of water and a good rest, so I flopped onto the bed as soon as I got home, with the fan on full blast. It did not take long, however, for the feeling of 'pins and needles' to start in my legs and I thought that I must have injured my back somehow, causing some pressure on the nerves. I resolved to keep resting, take some anti-inflammatories and see how things were in the morning. I couldn't stop my mind from wandering to other possible causes though, and oh, how I wished my housemate Jacqueline was not on home assignment in Holland at that moment! The night guard at my house was rather surprised to see how oddly I was walking when he came that evening, but I told him that I would probably feel better in the morning. That night, however, was completely without sleep; the strange feeling in my legs got worse, the backache deepened, my head hurt and, more worryingly, I could no longer urinate properly. I realized that these symptoms were reflecting a potentially serious problem with my spinal cord and my thoughts started racing as to all the possible diagnoses. Tumour? Guillain-Barré syndrome? Transverse myelitis? This was definitely not a simple back injury.

As soon as I could get myself together the next morning I somehow managed to get back on my bike and cycled to the hospital; riding a bike without being able to feel your legs is a rather bizarre experience, I discovered. I felt exhausted as I made my way to find Dr John and explained to him what was going on in my body. As we sat in his office I could see the concern on his face, which reflected what was also going on in my head. The relief of sharing it with someone else opened the way for my tears to flow. Within a few minutes, after gathering myself together again, I slowly made my way to the lab for blood and urine tests, then to get some X-rays and ultrasound scans done; all the while I could feel my legs getting weaker and weaker. The concern on my friends' faces as they took my blood and positioned me for the X-rays was breaking my heart. 'Mademoiselle Kerry, whatever has happened to you? You look so ill!'

By the end of the tests I could no longer walk on my own, so Dr John called his wife, Lesley, to come over to help me. We slowly staggered back to her house while we waited for the test results. By now the word was out that I wasn't doing well, and visitor after visitor came by to see what was going on. The truth was we didn't really know, and the test results were not able to shed much light on the situation either. As Dr John, I and the rest of our team talked it all over, it seemed that this was turning into a progressive neurological illness that we couldn't diagnose in Meskine without an MRI scan. The real danger was that it could start to affect my lungs, so that even breathing could become difficult. This was something that we definitely could not deal with, as we didn't have an intensive care facility with artificial ventilators in Meskine.

It was decided that my medical insurers needed to be contacted, so by that afternoon Scott and Dr John were on the phone talking to them and explaining the situation. There were also phone calls to my sending organization and family, keeping them informed of what was going on. All the while my legs were getting weaker and no longer felt as though they belonged to me; my head felt as if it was going to explode and my bladder just wasn't working any more, so a catheter had to be inserted. Finally the insurers decided that I needed to be medically evacuated to a more specialized hospital, but at that point they didn't know if it would be to South Africa or to the UK; either way, a plane would be coming to get me from the nearby airport in the morning. It had all happened so fast; within thirty-six hours my life had been turned upside down.

The following morning, after another stream of visits from friends and colleagues from the hospital, and after praying together with my team, I was carried out to the car and driven to find the plane. How grateful I was at that moment that Meskine was so near to an airport! And how grateful I was for such dear friends on my team who had become family to me; Scott and Lee, Dave and Patsy, and John and Lesley did everything to take care of me and get me on that plane. Ruth, who worked for Jacqueline and me in our home, also accompanied us to the airport. It was the most surreal parting I had ever had from these special people, not knowing if I was ever going to be able to come back to Meskine again. As I was carried up the steps into the waiting Learjet I felt as if I was being transported into another world, and the reality was just that. Ruth came up into the plane behind me and couldn't stop herself from looking shocked that this plane had come just to take me home. I could hardly believe it either. As we hugged each other tightly, cried together and said goodbye, it hit me that the rules for my medical care were just so different to hers. I get whisked off to the other side of the world, whereas if she had been dealt the same illness it would have been up to Meskine Hospital to take care of her. No neurologist. No intensive care unit. No MRI scan.

Fortunately, I was flown to the UK rather than South Africa, much to my relief and that of my family. Within days, it seems, hundreds of people began to pray for my healing around the world, but it was only afterwards that I realized just how many people had been prompted to pray by the Holy Spirit at that time. The following days, weeks and months were certainly life-changing for me in so many ways, and gave me a personal experience of how fragile our life's breath truly is. My need did indeed extend to intensive care and a ventilator for a couple of days, followed by lots of physiotherapy as I learned to walk again, but after two months I was discharged from hospital.

My neurologist finally diagnosed the illness as acute disseminating encephalomyelitis (ADEM) that had probably been caused by a virus. I am still learning lessons from this incredible experience, and I will remain grateful for these treasures for the rest of my earthly life. As my health improved, I was to be able to return briefly to Meskine fifteen months later, and then again a year later, to remain for many years. The story of how God gave me back my living breath, my legs, my vision and my strength is still at the front of my mind when I meet people who are experiencing a similar illness, and it has certainly made me a more compassionate physiotherapist. I'm grateful for medical insurance. I'm grateful for medical evacuations.

And I'm grateful to my God who heals, who daily carries our heavy loads and gives us joy in the morning.

Shouting for help and getting on a plane to a faraway land was not going to be the answer to a massive problem that was increasingly wrecking lives all around us, though. Just as in every other corner of the world, there was a plague that had also made its home on our doorstep.

8

An Epidemic Hidden in Shame

It had only been a few days since her life had been turned upside down. Finding herself a widow, left to raise her young daughter alone, Inna was struggling to settle her thoughts. Her husband had been unwell for a few months before coming to Meskine Hospital, getting weaker by the day. The family had hoped that there was something the doctors could do – surely some medication would sort him out, or maybe an operation of some kind. Sadly, Inna's husband faded away and died, the doctors apparently unable to help. Inna had been excluded from the discussions with the doctors, as her brothers-in-law had done all of that, and nobody was telling her what exactly her husband had died of. The culture of respecting your in-laws was such that Inna was too ashamed to ask the direct question that was prominent in her thoughts. 'Did my husband die of AIDS?' was the question that was troubling her. Now, a few days after her husband's funeral, Inna could not get the thought out of her mind.

Everyone knew that AIDS was incurable, which would explain the lack of communication from the family. 'His days were finished; this was God's will,' was about as much as Inna was told. Inna felt compelled to do her own research and started to look through some of her husband's belongings until she found some papers in an envelope that she hadn't seen before. Fortunately, she had done enough schooling to be able to read what was written and recognize them as medical documents. She flicked through them and then her heart almost stopped as she saw a lab result sheet. There it was, written clearly, her husband's name and the positive result for HIV. Stashed away in a plastic bag at the back of a drawer she also discovered a bottle of medication that she knew was the treatment given to people with HIV. Inna's world was tipped even more into turmoil now. What about her? And her little girl? Had her husband infected them with the virus? Were they also living under this death sentence? Panic, dread, anger and despair gripped Inna as she thought of the future . . .

The Western world was struck with the HIV/AIDS crisis in the 1980s but it took another decade for the horror to manifest itself in Cameroon. The spread of the disease here was mostly sexually transmitted among heterosexuals and, being a culture where having multiple partners is common either through polygamy or promiscuity, the speed of the epidemic was accelerated. At the time when MCWA was getting Meskine Hospital up and running in the mid-1990s, the measure and consequences of this disease were becoming apparent as more and more patients came for help. Initially, most were not from the village itself but from further afield, but this would change as the disease spread. By the time Dr Jacqueline Koster joined the team in 1998 the country had recognized that there was a serious HIV/AIDS epidemic underway and programmes to educate the population in prevention and seeking treatment were set up. As a general practitioner and already with many years of experience from working in Nigeria, Dr Jacqueline came to Meskine with the call and intention to be involved in community health work, so her arrival inevitably led her to join in with the local efforts of increasing public awareness of the HIV/AIDS situation.

At this time there was a laboratory test available in Meskine to diagnose the illness, so at least patients and blood donors could be screened to see if they were infected. This was not, however, as easy as it might seem. The general feeling among the local population was that they would prefer not to know whether they were infected and simply continue to live their lives in ignorance. This was rooted in the huge stigma that having the illness brought, as Inna's experience showed. Because it was sexually transmitted, it was seen to be extremely shameful to have the infection, the assumption being that you had brought this on yourself. It was seen as an illness that led to death, which was generally true in those days, as there was no treatment available in the far north of Cameroon yet. Most people just could not bear to find out that they had a death sentence hanging over their heads, such was the horror. It was therefore up to the doctors and nurses consulting the patients to take time and effort to explain the importance of being tested. At least if someone knew they had the illness it could prevent them from infecting anyone else.

As training programmes about the disease took off outside of the hospital in the village and surrounding areas, it echoed the increasing awareness being publicized on local radio and TV. Dr Jacqueline and her intrepid team methodically made their way around all the schools, teaching and discussing HIV/AIDS with teachers and students, highlighting the importance of prevention and helping to reduce the stigma. Jacqueline also visited all the local churches with the same agenda, and any other group in the neighbourhoods who were willing to listen.

Eventually the anti-retroviral (ARV) drug treatment became available for HIV/AIDS sufferers in the region. When it was finally distributed free of charge, the benefits of the drugs soon began to show and be understood as many benefited from increased quality of life. By 2012 Meskine Hospital was granted permission to distribute the drugs, and today it has a well-organized team that takes care of these patients, even carrying out follow-up visits to their homes, ensuring that as many as possible continue to 'live well' with the disease rather than die because of it.

The shame factor still hangs in the air though. It is often the unnamed illness, as if speaking out the words HIV/AIDS will invoke more doom and judgement. This secrecy and unwillingness to share information still means that it is a prevalent infectious disease, and the unwillingness to change behaviour of polygamy and promiscuity ensures that it will continue to be a menace in Cameroon for many years to come. The children who were infected by their mothers with the disease in the womb are now growing into adults, thanks to the drugs available, but the cloud of shame that hung over their parents is now sadly being passed on to them.

Inevitably, I also found myself involved in the lives of those living with the disease as people sought advice. Attending the funerals of those who had succumbed to the disease sadly became an all-too-regular occurrence, but not all lives were destroyed by it – for some it became an opportunity for change and hope.

Samira's story

When I first met Samira my Fulfulde was still in its early days, so deep conversation was very challenging and confusing, requiring maximum concentration. After a couple of months of preparation and building adjustments, I was ready to move off the hospital compound into a new home in the village; this quirky little house with no plumbing was to become home for Dr Jacqueline and me for the next twelve years. It turned out that Samira was going to be a regular visitor to this new home and we would become well-acquainted with each other over the following years. But I didn't first meet her at my home or in the street – the first time was at the hospital.

I was sitting on the ground next to the children's ward, chatting to a mother about her child who was hospitalized, probably due to the ubiquitous malaria. It was a typically hot day for that time of year with bright sunshine and I was sweating as usual, rather wishing I didn't have to wear the white coat that made every move feel so much hotter. I noticed my colleague from the tuberculosis department, known as 'Dr TB', wandering over to me, with his oft-furrowed brow, and medical notes in his hand. '*Mayramjo* (meaning 'Princess' – his playful, preferred name for me), I was wondering if I could talk to you for a minute.' As I got up off the mat on the ground, I excused myself from the woman I was chatting to. Dr TB and I wandered back across the sand to his office, my colleague talking as we walked. 'I have a lady here that I think you need to see. She has been having treatment for TB for a few weeks but has run out of money and is now unable to buy the medicine that she requires. She's still not very well and it seems she has no one in her family who is willing to step in. Is there anything we can do to help her? I'm afraid that, if we don't intervene, she will die.' And that was it, Samira came into my life.

When we got to his office there was this gaunt, very skinny, tall Pullo lady looking older than her early thirties years, with enormous eyes and a big smile. She did indeed still look very unwell; it seemed to me that a brisk wind could have blown her off her feet. She was dressed in a faded, multicoloured print wrapper skirt with matching head covering, a tired tee shirt hanging off her bony frame and a thin, grubby veil casually wrapped around her shoulders. I sat opposite her on a stool next to Dr TB's desk and started to flick through her medical notes. As we talked a bit more, I learned that Samira was a widow with two living children, two deceased, and sharing a home with her elderly parents. She had become increasingly unwell for a few months with a cough that would not go away, and she was losing weight at an alarming rate, now dipping under 40 kilos, with no appetite for eating.

Pulmonary TB had been diagnosed and in those days the medicine was not free of charge as it is now. The cost of 5,000 francs (around US$8) for the medicines each month became a considerable financial burden to many, as the treatment goes on for a minimum of six months. Much to Dr TB's frustration, patients would often not be able to finish the required drug therapy, as they ran out of money after a couple of months, and this in turn would contribute to the weakening of the effectiveness of the drugs overall. Mercifully for everyone, the government intervened with the help of the United Nations and reintroduced the policy for TB treatment to be distributed without charge from October 2002, but sadly this was too late for Samira. She explained that she had already sold all she had available to sell in order to buy the medication – her clothes, pots and pans, her jewellery. Now she just had one set of clothing left and had nothing else to sell. Could I help?

One of the advantages of being a privately managed hospital means MCWA is at liberty to waive the rules regarding money according to the patient's ability to pay the medical bills. It soon became clear as Meskine Hospital started to function that there would always be a group of people who desperately needed medical care but could not afford to pay for it, so out of this need a special fund that became known as the 'Poor Fund' was established. It is funded by generous supporters of MCWA who want to help by ensuring that nobody who needs it is refused medical treatment just because they are poor. Poverty has been defined by the United Nations as being without choices and opportunities.[1] It has been our experience in Meskine that this is so often the case when it comes to funding anything beyond the daily need to eat; even that can be an exhausting challenge for many. The Poor Fund enables Meskine Hospital to at least give a choice of receiving medical treatment to the most vulnerable in their time of need.

Over the years, the visiting team have learned to let our Cameroonian colleagues decide who are the people in genuine need of this help, as we are notoriously easily duped and unable to perceive the real situation! This time I saw the concern written on Dr TB's face; he could tell that Samira's need was very real, that she had come to the end of herself and no longer had any choices left. Dr TB wanted us to help her finish the treatment, as would the government department keeping watch over his shoulder to ensure that all TB patients complete the required drugs. Between us we had no qualms about sending her to administration to request Poor Fund help. My new friend was all smiles as she picked herself up and ambled off, grateful for this brief reprieve from the latest crisis to strike her.

As Samira wandered out of the office, Dr TB indicated for me to stay. He told me that today he wanted to send Samira for the routine HIV test that is offered to all TB patients, as the two diseases are so often linked, due to the weakened immune system. Dr TB had explained to her that it was wise to do this examination just to be sure of what was going on in her body. She had reluctantly agreed and went off to the lab to get this latest blood test done. As we parted, I thanked my colleague for going the extra mile to find help for Samira.

Later that afternoon, near to sunset, I was at home trying to rehydrate myself after another hot day at the hospital. I heard a light knock outside, and as I looked out of the window, I saw Samira's unmistakable big eyes peering at me over the top of the gate. I was rather surprised to see her again so soon. I invited her in and led her to my veranda where we sat down opposite each other. Somehow she seemed even taller and thinner than when I had seen her a few hours earlier. We took a few minutes to exchange the customary greetings as Samira got used to being alone in the presence of this white woman with strange Fulfulde. She had her medical booklet in her hands and the envelope that contained her HIV results. 'Dr TB told me to come and show you my results. I told him I know where your house is.'

'How did you know I lived here?' I asked rather quizzically.

'I've seen you moving your furniture in for the last few days; we know everything here!' she replied.

And that was my first lesson for living in my new neighbourhood; everyone would know every move I made from now on.

I took the envelope from Samira with a sinking feeling in my heart; there it was, clearly marked 'HIV positive', and so marked the beginning of a new season in Samira's life. As I explained the results to her, her big eyes started to brim over with tears which trickled over her prominent cheekbones. 'So does this mean I will die soon? No one gets better from this illness, right, doctor?' This was still quite early on in Cameroon's story with HIV and there was indeed great fear and pessimism about living with HIV/AIDS; the shame involved with being diagnosed with the disease meant that most people preferred to keep it to themselves, not even telling their closest relatives. This guarding of secrets was in fact one of the reasons for the high infection rates, as few were willing to reveal that they had the disease for fear of being ostracized and ridiculed.

It was no different for Samira; she was adamant that no one else should know about her illness. I explained about the future plan of ARV drugs to keep the disease under control that would mean life could still be lived. This treatment was not usually started in those days until the CD4 blood count got to a certain low level (sadly, too low and too late for many) so it was probable that Samira would not be eligible for the ARV drugs immediately, but there was at least hope. I explained the importance of finishing her TB treatment, eating well and refraining from sexual partners so as not to infect anyone else. All the time Samira was staring at me with those big eyes, her brow lined with sadness and her tired body slumped in the chair. 'Doctor, I know I'm going to die. What can I do? I've got young children and their father has already died. Who will take care of them? My parents are too old and my other people are far away.' It was all I could do to keep myself from crying with her, as I felt her pain and despair.

Somehow, I wanted to make things better but I was feeling out of my depth. I knew I had to do something, so I told Samira that she would be welcome at my home whenever she wanted to come and talk. I then offered to pray for her to know God's love and comfort at this difficult time. She peered at me through her tears, surprised by this offer and I wondered if she had understood me correctly.

'Did you say you want to pray for me?'

'Errr, yes, I did', and I put my hands out in front of me with my palms up to indicate what I meant.

'Oh, I get it! Yes, that's fine, please do.'

I wondered if I had used the wrong word for 'pray', but whatever, Samira agreed. I did not find praying in Fulfulde very easy yet, but I managed to mumble something and she seemed grateful. As we finished, I felt an inner nudge to invite Samira to come and see me again and asked her if she wanted to hear about Jesus, the One who carried our diseases.[2] 'Next time you come, would you like to hear more about him?'

She nodded and said, 'See you next time, doctor.'

It was hard to see her leave with a heavy heart. I could only imagine the inner turmoil that she was experiencing as she returned home that evening, not feeling able to talk to anyone else about this life-changing news.

Our next encounter was only a few days later, and I began to share the good news about Jesus with Samira. It's not always obvious to know where to start with the message, so I tried to find out what Samira already knew. Like all Fulbe children, she had attended qur'anic school from about the age of 5, but she herself confessed that, 'I have a hard head and can't learn things well,' so I realized it was best to go slowly. Her knowledge of the Qur'an was minimal. She certainly had never heard anything about Jesus, as far as she could remember, and had never learned to read. I started with the story of creation and how sin separated people from God, and could tell that her retention of information was not very good. Repetition and simple story-telling would probably be the most effective way, but my Fulfulde wasn't good enough yet to tell the stories without the words in front of me, so it was quite a slow process. After a couple of visits and stories I decided to jump over most of the Old Testament and fast-track to stories about Jesus. Frankly, I thought I needed to get on with this message because I didn't actually know if Samira was going to make it more than a few weeks or months, as she was so thin and frail.

After exchanging several visits we got to know each other better and were able to talk quite freely, especially since Samira had become used to my rather disjointed Fulfulde. Little by little, she started to look and feel better as her appetite returned. Her family and neighbours started to remark to her that she was making an amazing recovery, much to their surprise, as the general thought in the neighbourhood was that Samira was going to die soon. When someone is so ill for so long it can only be assumed that their days are almost finished, but it seemed that God had other plans for Samira. One of the happiest people to see this gradual recovery was Dr TB. For those who work in the medical profession, there is no greater joy at work than seeing your patient regain their health; these are the moments we treasure. Samira never really regained her full weight and has always looked rather underfed, but you could always tell how she was feeling by the way she walked. When she was well her walk was forthright and her body straight, with her head held high; when she was feeling unwell, her movement was less assured and her head bowed down. Over those following months we began to see her head rise again, but it took a while longer for her stride to become more assured.

Samira's special day is clearly etched on my memory. She had come to visit one evening to hear more from the Bible about Jesus. As usual, we were sitting on the mat on the floor in my lounge. It was dry season and dust hung in the air. It didn't seem to matter how often you wiped down surfaces in the house, within minutes there was a fine layer of dust on them again, so the mat always had this dusty smell and feel to it. We propped ourselves up against the chairs behind us, this being the preferred function of chairs in Meskine, rather than for sitting on. Stretching your legs out on a mat was always preferable to having to sit on a chair, 'I'm too tired to sit on a chair' being the oft-repeated phrase.

This evening's story was the Prodigal Son from Luke 15. I read the story to Samira a couple of times, then she repeated it back in her own words, with ample encouragement from me. Gradually we got through it and then came her question.

'Kerry, do you think God could ever forgive me, just like the father forgave his son in this story? I've done terrible things, too, and I don't know if God will forgive what I have done. What do you think?'

It was one of those moments when time seemed to stand still as I heard her question, and my heart leapt within me. For the first time, Samira was revealing her longing to know what God thought of her sin and what could be done about it. It was true, her life had been far from perfect, just like all our lives, and had even led to this life sentence of having HIV/AIDS. Now this story of compassion and grace touched her heart so much that she wanted it for herself. And so it was that I was able to hang the good news about Jesus on this hook in such a way that she could grasp it. She understood that Jesus had paid for her sin so that she could be forgiven and made new. That evening Samira said 'yes' to Jesus with joy and relief. It was very much like a child coming to her father, saying sorry and asking to start afresh.

In many ways Samira's faith has remained childlike and her spiritual growth has been minimal in our eyes. But if you ask her today who Jesus is to her, she will tell you, 'He is the One who died for me; he is the One who hears my prayers; he is the One who has kept me alive to see my children grow up.' There have indeed been numerous times when we thought that Samira's earthly life was near the end but, incredibly, she has recovered her strength each time and even lived to see her grandchildren. Poverty is her constant companion, but she has experienced the presence of God in her darkest times and met Jesus there. In many ways her life is disorganized and lurches from one crisis to another, so typical of many we have come into contact with in Meskine. However, right in the middle of it all, Jesus walked in.

It makes me wonder, sometimes, what happened to many of those others we hear of briefly in the gospels who met Jesus, such as the woman healed of bleeding, the blind beggars given back their sight, the lepers cleansed, others delivered from evil spirits. How many of them were like Samira: poor, hungry, despairing and dying – not important in the world's eyes, maybe even suffering because of bad choices they had made? Then they met Jesus and something was made better in their lives, like a waft of fresh air coming into a stuffy room, or coming up for breath when you are drowning. They may not have understood every wonderful thing about Jesus, or what it means to be 'born again'[3] in every respect of their new life with him. They may not even have realized the incredible ongoing grace that Jesus poured into their lives, but they did know and experience that he is kind and good at the moment they were healed, and that life was better with him than without him.

Samira's life continued to be one of precariousness, and bad choices were still made that exacerbated her problems. It was hard for her to break old habits, as the mentality of 'whatever happens is God's will' contributed to a lifetime of repeated irresponsibility. But there was always something in her that drew her back to Jesus – that remembrance of the father welcoming back his wayward child. When some in the community around her began to suspect that she had 'gone into the church' because I was visiting her, they started to intimidate and threaten her.

Even though she had never set foot in the church, she found this pressure frightening and daunting, her worst fear being that there would be no one willing to bury her body when she died if the community thought she had become a Christian. She waited until her elderly mother had passed away before getting baptized. Her mother had requested that she do this, as she couldn't bear the shame of her daughter becoming a follower of Jesus. Samira's baptism was carried out alongside those of a handful of other new believers from a Muslim background one evening, under the cover of darkness, at a quiet end of the hospital grounds. It was a simple ceremony to celebrate how Almighty God stoops down and touches a broken life with the person of Jesus.

My physiotherapy work soon taught me that it was not only HIV that was ruining lives with such devastation. Rather than a gradual decline of ill health that often petered out into death, there was another uninvited companion that turned up without warning and with unexpected speed.

9

Learning to Walk Again

Yusuf's story

After the MCWA team's exodus from Meskine in 2014 we relocated a day's drive further south where it was safer for foreigners. Being new in town and expecting more team members to join us in a few months' time, we asked for help in finding houses to rent. One of the houses we viewed was nearby to a Pullo man named Yusuf. When we had finished viewing the house our guide, having learned that we had come from Meskine Hospital, asked us to come and see his friend Yusuf, who lived a few doors down the road and needed some help.

Yusuf's family were mostly truck drivers and had been based in CAR for many years, although they were originally from Cameroon. When civil war erupted in CAR, Yusuf's family were caught in the middle of it, like so many thousands of others. Eventually they all left and moved back to Cameroon, but not before Yusuf's life was changed forever. One day he was shot by a random bullet that was aimed into a crowd. As it ripped through his chest he collapsed to the ground, shattering his spine. He immediately felt as though an implosion had taken place in his body and found that he could no longer move his legs. This began a long journey of hospitalization, first in CAR, then in Cameroon. By the time we met Yusuf he had already spent a total of two years in different hospitals trying to find a way to get better. He was now home with his family who were taking great care of him, even finding a wheelchair for him. But Yusuf was weak, depressed and covered in sores from sitting and being in bed so much. He asked if Meskine Hospital could help him. We were pleased to say yes, knowing that our staff could help get his stubborn pressure sores better, and the physiotherapy team could help him to get stronger so he could have better balance when he was sitting. At this time, Yusuf could not be left alone while sitting as he was so weak and couldn't save himself if he lost his balance.

After much discussion and thought, the family agreed to send Yusuf on the long journey up to Meskine Hospital as one last effort to help him. Financially, they were becoming exhausted with all the demands that Yusuf's situation had put on them, but we reassured them that we would keep the cost down as much as possible. The MCWA staff were ready right from the start to welcome him and make him feel at home. The doctors, surgical team and ward nurses all set to work on getting his wounds cleaned up. The physiotherapy team also started working with Yusuf to get his arms and upper-body strength going. With this renewed effort, encouragement and social interaction, Yusuf's mood lightened and he burst into life. After a couple of months, Yusuf's desire and motivation to learn to walk became apparent, so after much debate and discussion, the team decided to go ahead and work towards this high goal of teaching Yusuf to walk again. He had no voluntary muscle activity at all below his ribcage, but his arms were really strong by now and he could sit without falling over.

The next stage, however, would be very challenging. It required learning to stand with metal braces strapped to his legs, developing enormous strength and technique to lift his body upwards and forwards, followed by his heavy legs and then moving the walking frame forwards. All these things would require hard work and motivation. Yusuf had plenty of this and determination to go with it. Hours of physical effort day after day, encouragement from his family and hospital staff, and extensive teamwork finally enabled Yusuf to leave our hospital two years later, standing tall and walking short distances with his leg braces and walking frame.

Yusuf's story illustrates beautifully how the hospital team came together to help him reach his goal: nurses, doctors, physiotherapists, radiology, laboratory, administration, guards, pharmacy, orthopaedic workshop technicians and cleaners. Because of this joint sense of 'ownership' of Yusuf's success it was not surprising that, on the day he finally left hospital to return home, there was a very emotional scene. Yusuf had made many new friends among the staff who had given of themselves to help him. Everyone knew his little girl, who had grown up for two years on the hospital compound. His wife and sister had become known at the market because they had been there for so long. Even people in the village of Meskine had got to know Yusuf and heard that 'the man whose legs don't work has learned to walk again'. Yusuf had decided that he wanted to learn to walk and that he would not go home until the job was done. Finally, the day had come and he could go home, knowing he had achieved what he set out to do. Along the journey he had gained some new forever friends for whom he would be grateful for the rest of his life.

As a physiotherapist, I have found that some of the hardest patients to treat and help in Cameroon have been people who have become paralysed. This challenge has not been anything to do with the people themselves as, for the most part, they are the bravest and most motivated of all, like Yusuf. Rather, the struggle comes from the circumstances and frustratingly few options that are available to help them to get on with life. Finding yourself facing the rest of your life without the use of your legs is a life-shattering moment, and then discovering that it will be a lifelong uphill struggle from then on is truly exhausting.

In the more developed world there are myriads of aids and helps to make life easier, such as special beds, hoists, mobility aids and all kinds of gadgets; there are wonderful rehabilitation centres to help people make the transition to life in a wheelchair and help them get back to work and a social life; public transport and buildings are increasingly more useable for those who can't get about on their legs. All these things that we foreigners have come to take for granted are just not available in Cameroon. Even getting a wheelchair is a massive challenge. So the lot of someone who suddenly finds themselves paralysed is a sorry one.

Sadly, the incidence of people becoming paralysed is high in Cameroon, and Meskine Hospital has received its share of people coming to us in this predicament. One of the top ten causes of premature death in Cameroon is road traffic accidents;[1] the roads are poorly maintained, as are many of the vehicles on them, and any kind of highway code is often ignored. Crushed and twisted spines are therefore a frequent consequence of those who survive a terrible road accident, rendering their legs and sometimes their arms weak and even useless. The high incidence of tuberculosis of the spine also leaves many with long-term neurological damage and paralysis, especially when diagnosis and therefore treatment has been delayed.

What contributes to the complications of life with paralysis is the long list of secondary issues that arise. Being unable to stand, and for some even to sit, means that excessive pressure is put on the bony parts of the pelvis and hips which leads to deep sores that become infected and, consequently, difficult to heal. Being unable to feel the pain that these wounds would cause if normal sensation were present means that people often stay for hours on end in the same position with no relief given to the fragile area. Along with paralysis of the limbs comes reduced or loss of control of the bladder and bowel. This is particularly hard to come to terms with, and it takes a long time for people to create a routine and way of managing. Most people end up with a permanent catheter to control the urine, and this in itself is a huge risk for repeated infections.

Loss of financial independence for many is heartbreaking. For those who were previously young, vigorous, healthy and working to meet their own needs and the needs of their family, this is particularly stressful. Who will provide the food now? What about the children and their school fees? How long will I be a financial burden on my family with all these medical bills? These are the questions that go around in their minds daily.

Social isolation in the long term gradually begins to take its toll too. Being unable to get out of the house and interact without being dependent on others, or simply being dependent on some form of mobility aid, means that you are often excluded from the day-to-day hubbub of being part of society. Unless others choose to visit you in your home or you keep your phone close by, you become locked in to a lonelier life than you would have wished for.

It is indeed a difficult road that those who find themselves paralysed have to travel. But some, like Yusuf, have made a remarkable impression on the team at Meskine Hospital and have added to the colourful history of those who left us much better off than when they first arrived.

Abdou's Story

Tuberculosis is a destructive, life-sapping scourge that continues to create rack and ruin across sub-Saharan Africa, and Cameroon is no exception. Our hospital has been a life-saving sanctuary for many who find themselves with a TB diagnosis. The majority have been those with pulmonary TB affecting their lungs, but this disease is also prolific in the bones, intestines and other tissues. Because of its sinister nature, the symptoms are often vague and generalized at the beginning of the illness, so many patients do not get a positive TB diagnosis until they are already very weak and unwell. Tuberculosis is regularly left undiagnosed for far too long. This was the case with Abdou.

Abdou was a young, healthy man who lived in a vibrant fishing community. He was doing well, contributing to the welfare of his family as a fisherman, just like so many of his friends. Fish is a very popular source of protein in Cameroon, so there is always a good market for it. Sadly for Abdou, his part in this trade was drastically changed when he was struck by TB in his spine.

By the time Abdou had found his way to Meskine Hospital he was already paralysed because the TB had attacked the thoracic vertebrae in his spinal column, causing compression of his spinal cord. The X-ray clearly showed the typical wedge-shaped destruction of the bones and the now misaligned spine. But the compression on his spinal cord was partial rather than complete, creating incredibly strong spasms in his legs that he couldn't control. His legs were no longer supple but were disobedient and often rigid. It was difficult for him to get into a comfortable position either lying on a bed or sitting up because his legs would refuse to bend or would jump around uncontrollably. His legs no longer felt as though they belonged to him but gave him a burning sensation with a constant 'pins and needles' feeling.

Along with these symptoms, Abdou had lost his dignity and his confidence, as he needed help from his family to do everything. He did not have enough balance and strength to sit up and eat unless someone helped him, not to mention taking care of his personal needs. It was not exactly clear how long Abdou had been suffering with TB, but his was a typical story of feeling tired and weak, which gradually developed into loss of appetite and an aching back, followed by growing weakness in his legs until he could no longer walk. As was often the case, if only the diagnosis of TB in the spine had been made earlier, Abdou might never have become paralysed. The previous medical investigations he had received before coming to us had not been helpful in finding the cause of his problems.

But, like Yusuf, Abdou was another determined young man. He was ready to do anything to get his legs functioning again and be able to return to fishing. With the appropriate medication, the dedication of his family taking care of him and the encouragement of the hospital staff, Abdou gradually became stronger. His sitting balance improved as the muscles in his upper body grew strong again. He began to gain control of the strong muscle spasms in his legs too, but he was not satisfied with the extent of progress he had made. All Abdou wanted was to walk again.

Scott met Abdou for the first time when he was wandering through the men's ward having visited another patient. As he walked past Abdou's bed he was met with a friendly smile, so Scott stopped to greet him and they started chatting. The next day Scott visited Abdou again and gave him an MP3-player to listen to Bible stories, explaining that, if he liked it, he could keep it with him to hear all one hundred of the lessons. An hour later, when Scott passed by again, he found Abdou still with the headphones on. He smiled and gave Scott a 'thumbs up' sign, indicating that he was enjoying what he was hearing. From that time on, Scott and the chaplains visited Abdou daily and discussed what he was listening to. The lessons were gradually explaining God's plan to send the Messiah right from the beginning of history; Abdou realized early on that this was alluding to Jesus, even before he heard the lessons from the gospels. It did not take long for Abdou to be ready to embrace Jesus for himself while he was at the hospital.

One morning, as Scott was alone at home and praying for Abdou, he had an inner nudge and conviction that he had not experienced before. The thought would not go away and Scott felt he had to act upon it. He was feeling convicted to pray for Abdou to 'rise up and walk' in the way that Jesus modelled to his disciples in the gospels, and in the way that Peter and John acted in Acts.[2] After a couple of days of considering this and praying some more, Scott went to sit with Abdou and his mother outside in the shade and read to them from Acts 3, the story of the paralysed man who was healed. Scott asked Abdou if he had faith that Jesus could heal him in the same way; without hesitation Abdou answered yes. So, as the three of them sat there, Scott quietly prayed asking Jesus to heal Abdou's legs so that he could walk again. When he had finished he looked at Abdou and, taking his hand, he said, 'In the name of Jesus, Abdou, get up and walk!'

With his heart pounding in his chest and with great hope and expectation, Scott waited to see how Abdou was doing . . . Abdou tried to get up and Scott helped out to see if he could stand on his legs. 'Do you feel anything different in your legs, Abdou? Has your strength come back?' It was obvious that nothing had changed and Scott couldn't hide his disappointment. Abdou expressed his deep gratitude to Scott for praying and quickly announced that this was God's will for him, and it should be accepted. Scott came home that evening knowing that he had been obedient to what he felt God had asked him to do, but still that question was hanging in the air, 'Why didn't Abdou get up out of that wheelchair and start walking around?'

In the weeks that followed it seemed that Abdou would not be going home walking, but he had certainly regained his strength. As a final gesture of help, Meskine Hospital was able to send him home with a hand-propelled tricycle which would at least give Abdou some independence and means of getting back to some kind of work. He received it very gratefully and soon became an expert tricyclist.

A few months later, Scott and one of the chaplains made the four-hour journey to visit Abdou, to see how he was doing. Abdou had gone home with the audio Bible lessons and had been sharing them with his family too, but when his uncle heard about it, he became very angry and threatened to beat Abdou if he ever found him listening to them again. Abdou was shocked, as he was not expecting such an angry reaction, leaving him with little choice other than to stop listening to the lessons that had given him so much joy. He was, after all, still completely dependent on his family for his needs. After some time being at home and getting stronger, Abdou was able to get back to work, not as a fisherman but, with the use of his tricycle, he took himself off to the market and cooked chickens to sell. He was grateful to have gained some independence again.

As time went on it became harder to stay in touch with Abdou, as he didn't have a phone and lived far away. But then, out of the blue a couple of years later, Abdou contacted the chaplains at the hospital with the most joyful news. Abdou wanted to return the tricycle that MCWA had given him as he no longer needed it. He was now able to walk! The prayer of faith that Scott had offered had finally been answered. Abdou had learned to walk again, he was on his feet at last. Not only that, but Abdou confirmed that he still had Jesus in his heart and never stopped believing in him, despite the opposition from his family. How often we question God when we don't see the answers to our prayers when we think they should be answered. Abdou's story is a lesson to us that sometimes what seems like an unanswered prayer is in fact a 'not yet' and that God has not finished because he is still working his purposes out.

Gabriel's Story

The timing of the return of Abdou's tricycle was perfect for another young man's benefit. I had known Gabriel since he was 2 years old, first meeting him when I was visiting a friend in his neighbourhood in Meskine. She asked me to come and see her neighbour's little boy as something had gone wrong with his legs. I found a lovely boy, but indeed his legs were not functioning as they should. They were hanging limp when they should have been running around. His mother explained that he had learned to walk the same way as all his brothers and sisters had, but then gradually stopped walking a few months later, and a lump had appeared on his back. I had a quick look under his shirt and there it was, the tell-tale sign of TB in the spine: a hard, bony protuberance from a collapsed vertebra beneath the skin. This little boy's legs had become paralysed just when he was enjoying his newly learned freedom of walking.

Gabriel's mother brought him to the hospital the next day, where an X-ray confirmed my suspicions of TB. He started the six-month programme of medication, and I worked with him to try to get his legs functioning again. Happily, Gabriel's legs did get stronger over time and he began to stand and walk with a walking frame, then crutches as he got older. But things would change again as Gabriel grew taller. In Europe or the USA, he would have been a candidate for an operation to reinforce his spine with internal metal fixation, acting as scaffolding while he grew so that his spine would be strong and straight. Gabriel's spine, however, was still not straight and, as he got bigger, the deformity in his spine became more pronounced.

Eventually, by the time he was around 12 years old, his spinal cord became injured again as his spinal column collapsed around it. Gabriel was now completely paralysed, with no movement or feeling in his legs at all. He was not able to go to school like the rest of his siblings and his life became housebound. To pass the time and earn some money, Gabriel taught himself to mend shoes and buckets by repairing the rubber and plastic, and to make carpets by sewing grain sacks together. He was skilled with his hands and not one to sit around doing nothing, even though he was forced to drag himself on the ground in the dust.

At the time when Abdou returned his tricycle to Meskine Hospital, Gabriel immediately came to my mind as the next person who could benefit from it. The orthopaedic workshop team got to work, renovating it with fresh paint, new tyres, new cushions and some grease. Gabriel was 17 years old by now and resigned to a life at home, crawling around on the ground, never to be free. When we went to tell him that we had a gift of a tricycle for him, he could hardly contain his joy. Finally, some good news! The very next day he came with his mother to the hospital to try it out and learn how to use it. With a few alterations and another day of training, he was ready to head home with his new set of wheels and independence. It was a beautiful day to see Gabriel and his mother leaving the hospital, all smiles and thankfulness because, in his heart, Gabriel had got a measure of his legs back again. This tricycle would extend his boundaries, allowing him to go to the market to repair shoes and sell his carpets, to go to church, to socialize with people his own age and allow him to choose where he spent his days. Learning to walk for Gabriel had not been possible, but learning to be independent has, and for him this tricycle was a life-changer.

Jebba's story

When paralysis of limbs is caused by trauma or disease, there is some degree of resignation that it was beyond the control of human power to prevent it entirely, but effort and care can make the future manageable for the one incapacitated. When the paralysis is caused by human error and carelessness, however, I have often found myself raging on the inside and struggling to control my words of condemnation. Sadly, we have received many patients over the years who have come to Meskine Hospital with withered legs caused by health workers at other clinics and hospitals. Basic training for nurses in how to administer injections and where in the body to give them should ensure that precious nerves are not damaged as the needle is inserted. The human anatomy does not vary from one to another a great deal, so one would think it should not be difficult for student nurses to learn these basics, if they are taught it. It only takes an injection into a muscle to be misplaced by a centimetre or two to ruin a life forever. This is what happened to Jebba when she was a little girl.

As a toddler, she was suffering with severe malaria and was taken by her family to a local health centre, where quinine injections were prescribed and administered directly into her gluteal muscle and thigh. Having recently learned to walk, she was suddenly subjected to a life of immobility in an instant, as her nerves were stabbed and ruined by the needles, rendering her leg paralysed. She could no longer control her hip, knee or ankle and stopped walking. As she got older the rest of her body grew but the affected leg became thinner as it atrophied from disuse, resembling a withered branch hanging limply under her clothes. By the time she was an adult her foot could no longer touch the ground as the knee had become fixed in a bent position; as a result, Jebba had become housebound. She could stand perfectly well on her strong good leg but she had never walked again since those injections when she was a child. Jebba had become accustomed to crawling around on the ground, the callouses on her hands and knees telling her story.

Jebba was a shy woman who rarely raised her voice and certainly would not initiate a conversation. I wondered how much of this introversion was actually her character and how much was a consequence of living a shattered life. Her home life had not been ideal, as her parents had split up when she was very young; she had stayed with her father but was then passed on to an aunt, who was not an easy woman to live with. Living under the authority of this domineering, unhappy woman did not inspire or encourage Jebba out of her shell. Jebba had been given in marriage to an older man as a young teenager, the assumption being it would be better for her to be married and have children than to remain a burden to her family. After all, she could cook and wash clothes even if she could not go to the well to draw water or plough a field. The marriage did not last, as he was a cruel man and, when Jebba's first child died as a baby, she was sent back to her aunt. This was when I was introduced to her.

Jebba's aunt was our neighbour and invited me in to meet her niece. 'Kerry, as you are a leg doctor, can't you do something to help my girl? Nobody else will marry her while she is like this.'

As I looked behind her, there was Jebba sitting on the sand at the entrance to their home; her veil was pulled slightly over her face, but an expression of curiosity was peering out at me. We went into the little grass-roofed house behind her and, after we had exchanged greetings, I asked Jebba what had happened to her legs; the story came tumbling out. I could tell that Jebba was a healthy young woman, even if rather thin, and she had one very strong leg that could carry her.

'So, Jebba, why have you never learned to walk with crutches?' I thought this would have been something she had at least tried in the twenty years since her leg became paralysed.

'Well, no one has ever given me any crutches to try and I know I would never be able to afford them if I came to the hospital.' And that was the simple truth. Lack of money, lack of knowledge and lack of initiative on the part of her family had kept Jebba in the dust for two decades.

The reality was that our crutches were not that expensive compared to those from other hospitals in the area, and her family would have been able to afford them if they had wanted to get them for Jebba. Even she might have been able eventually to save enough money from the meagre income she made from sewing to get them for herself. They did not know, however, until now, that this was even possible.

A few days later I welcomed Jebba to the hospital and measured her up for her first pair of crutches. After some training sessions on how to use them, Jebba proudly walked out of the physiotherapy department with her newly acquired independence to find a motorbike taxi to take her home. The sense of accomplishment that she felt that day gave her confidence, and the next time I saw her, there was the biggest smile on her face. She met me at the entrance of her home, standing tall and able to greet me face to face and eye to eye rather than having to look up at me from the ground. Her sense of dignity was coming back. As is often the way in Meskine, good news for one person is celebrated by the many, so on that visit I could sense the happiness in her aunt and the rest of the family. They were genuinely delighted to see Jebba up and about on her crutches. If only they had known a few years earlier how easy it was . . .

It was not unusual for me to find people like Jebba in the village who could benefit from some physiotherapy advice as I visited in the neighbourhood. I would also enjoy following up some of my hospital patients after they went home, if they were from Meskine or not too far away. It was always a privilege to be welcomed into these homes as a friend; hospitality of the Fulbe is second to none. Occasionally, though, follow-up visits at home took on a whole different dimension when it involved semi-nomadic Fulbe friends from the bush.

10

Baby Jesus in the Bush

Bump! Bump! Scrape! Rattle! That was the sound of our car as it approached the hidden-away village of the semi-nomadic Fulbe people who had become our friends. There was only a footpath to access them, so the thorns, tall grass and rocks were not used to this punishment from a heavy vehicle. Once we pushed our way through, there were the grass roofs and mud houses looking rather abandoned. None of them had any doors, and furniture consisted of cane bed frames and a cane ledge to store pots and pans. Signs of life emerged as our car was seen. Little children from all directions started running towards us, big smiles on their faces, shouting, '*Kerry 'en ngari! Kerry 'en ngari!*' roughly meaning 'Kerry and her lot have come!' We never got tired of this excited, warm welcome.

The Fulbe people in the far north of Cameroon have mostly become settled in towns and villages like Meskine. They have lost their huge herds of cattle and have learned to farm. Most of our neighbours would call themselves Fulbe but they have never owned a cow, let alone milked one, and are children of mixed parentage. But the Fulbe out in the bush remain 100 per cent pure. It is the welfare of their cattle that is the priority as the herd is their pride and joy; everything else is second-ary to this. They are so orientated to protecting the family's herds that they will marry their direct cousins. Family relationships are therefore very complicated. Your aunt or uncle is also your in-law; you are a nephew or niece as well as the parent of the grandchildren. There is also a very strong sense of being together, living as a community and never as an individual. Some bush Fulbe still have facial or skin markings that represent which specific family clan they belong to, such is the importance of family identity.

We got to know these precious people because one of their sons was born without an anal opening, a congenital deformity known as imperforate anus. He was born in the bush while his family were out for a few months with the cattle. This is a life with no house, no bed, hardly any water, no shops, just open fields and lots and lots of dust. The little boy was named Iisa, which is Arabic for Jesus. By his sixth day, the family realized something was very wrong with Iisa, so they brought him to our hospital; by now he was a very sick boy with an obstructed abdomen as he was unable to pass any stool.

Dr Carsten carried out emergency surgery for a colostomy to relieve his immediate symptoms. This was not, however, a long-term solution to the problem, especially considering his family's lifestyle out in the bush with their cows. Keeping him free from infection, getting regular access to colostomy bags and enabling this little boy to thrive would be a constant challenge if he was left like this. Something else needed to be done. Dr Carsten decided it would be best to send Iisa for specialist surgery to construct an anus, thus removing the need for a colostomy bag altogether. Unfortunately, the procedure would have to be done at a bigger hospital at the other end of Cameroon as we couldn't do it, at that time, in Meskine.

With the generous help of the Willing and Abel organization, Iisa and his parents embarked on the journey of a lifetime;

not by foot or donkey as they had been used to, but by bus, train and taxi. Suddenly this family was plunged into the bizarre world of hospitals, beds, rooms with doors, paperwork, people dressed in white coats and being surrounded by people speaking every language other than Fulfulde. Mbingo Baptist Hospital was their destination. Being situated up in the beautiful hills of the north-west province, Iisa's family discovered a significantly cooler climate than the far north. Feeling cold all the time was probably one of the biggest hardships for them during their stay there. God answered many prayers during this trip, and the family came back with their healthy, repaired boy, relieved and so thankful.

Iisa still needed some medical follow-up, and that's when we started to visit them more regularly in their village where the 'settled' part of the family lived. Each week a couple of us would make the thirty-minute drive out of Meskine and receive a joyful welcome every time. The settled part of the family consisted of the older grandmothers who were not strong enough to travel with the cows any more, and some of the young mothers with their children who preferred not to travel but took care of the older generation. There was a rotation of men who would come back to the village to check up on everyone, but most of the male teenagers, husbands and fathers would stay with the herd. There were still a few animals that remained in the village: some cows to provide milk, goats and chickens, and a couple of donkeys to help bring water from the well.

Whenever we arrived, we were met with the welcoming entourage of women and children of various sizes, all of whose feet seemed to be immune to thorns and rocks as they ran over to us barefoot. They then grabbed our hands and escorted us to one of the grandmother's huts, stretched out a grass woven mat for us to sit on the hard ground and everyone gathered to see what these strange white people had to say this week. There were the usual greetings as every adult present took turns to greet every other adult. When it came to our turn, they would switch to simpler Fulfulde, making sure we could understand. It was a steep learning curve for us on these visits as we were exposed to the intricacies and depths of this already difficult language that we never heard in Meskine.

When the greetings were done, there would be the medical questions. We usually found someone who was unwell, a child failing to thrive or a question about medication that had been bought at the market. It was always a relief to have Dr Jacqueline with us on these visits, her knowledge being indispensable as we tried to diagnose the bizarre symptoms that were described to us: a young pregnant woman eating dirt, a grandmother's heart 'bursting', 'the worms in my stomach are hungry', or 'my whole body hurts' . . . Then finally something more straightforward: 'I think my ears are blocked.' On the next visit Dr Jacqueline brought her otoscope to check out the offending ears, much to the entertainment and fascination of all, and suddenly everybody wanted to be looked at, so they developed 'blocked ears' too.

At some point during the visit we would be brought some fresh milk to drink. To some of our team this was perfectly fine and even tasty, but to others of us it was another one of those things that you just have to learn to do because it is the loving thing. Fulbe are wonderfully generous hosts. Giving their visitors something to eat or drink is a sign that they are very welcome, so refusing to dine on what is presented to you is considered very impolite and even offensive. It was therefore non-negotiable when the calabash bowl of milk was presented to us; it must be consumed! It was usually warm and had that odour that tells you the cow is not too far away. Along with the milk came the flies, perched around the rim of the bowl, but with a gentle waft of the hand they would be temporarily displaced. Trying to keep my face neutral and not telling of the horror I was feeling inside, I learned to guzzle the milk down, managing not to gag. I was always glad to have a companion with me who enjoyed the milk so they could drink the greater share!

After all of this, we soon settled into a routine of sharing stories from the Bible with our friends, using pictures to help. None of them could read, so they had never been able to understand the Qur'an for themselves, and had never seen a Bible. They had been taught the fundamentals of Islam however, and were keen adherents of the five-times-a-day prayers and the fasting month of Ramadan. Even so, they were excited to be hearing about the prophets of old. Starting at the beginning of the gospel story, we worked our way from Creation, through the Old Testament and finally to the stories of Jesus. It was an incredible privilege to be invited to share these stories with them, and for sure it was the first time that they had been heard by our friends.

It was an experience repeated every time we came. Imagine a grass-roofed mud house about 4 metres square crammed with 20 people, all sitting on the dirt, sweat pouring down our faces, flies buzzing, chickens wandering in and out, children wriggling and fighting for position, all eyes fixed on the picture being held and most of the ears listening to the story being told. Some of the women would repeat the story phrase by phrase in their more complicated Fulfulde to the grandmothers. The children would be struck by something in the picture and want to know more about it. After the story was told we then asked them to retell it to us to make sure they had understood. Little by little, we worked our way through the stories in this way.

As we approached the end of the stories about Jesus, we brought the *Jesus* film for them to watch as a way of drawing the overall message together. For people in the modern world these days it would be difficult for someone to remember what the first film was that they ever saw. We grow up watching the TV and movies, so it's not a special event at all. For these Fulbe, the first film they ever saw was the *Jesus* film, and probably the first time they ever saw a screen. They actually ended up seeing it five times in their own language, such was their enjoyment of it. We took it out to them on a portable DVD player; twenty faces all crowded around the small screen, many of them listening intently. By the third viewing they were starting to be able to repeat the dialogue and excitedly anticipate what was coming next. The most memorable reaction was when Jesus appeared after his resurrection and one of the grandmas watching exclaimed, '*A jabbaama!*' meaning 'welcome'. After the horror and sadness of the crucifixion, there was a real sense of relief and joy that Jesus was alive again.

During this time of storying and sharing the gospel with Iisa's family we know that the wonder of Jesus had touched them, as their discussions and retention of the stories revealed. We also know that there was some opposition to us sharing with the women. We particularly noticed a change in the attentiveness of some of the women after a qur'anic teacher had stayed with them for a few weeks during Ramadan. Had he told them to stop listening to us? Had he warned them or threatened them? We don't know. But we do know that the gospel is powerful to change lives forever. We are thankful that a little baby called Iisa opened the way for us to befriend this family and share about another person called Jesus.

Baby Iisa grew up to be a lovely, healthy boy and a constant reminder to his family that for a season they heard about *Iisa*

Almasiihu, Jesus Christ. It remains our hope and prayer for these Fulbe that, one day, this whole clan will say 'welcome' to Jesus as their Lord and their Good Shepherd.[1]

Jamilla's story

Over the years, Meskine Hospital has been visited by many other Fulbe from the bush like Iisa's family, but there are some visitors who make a deeper impression on the team than others. Jamilla was one of those.

Jamilla was a typically lithe young woman, with no extra weight on her slender frame. Her dark hair was neatly braided in thin rows that extended down the back of her neck, with gold earrings dangling to enhance her bright face. A smile was never far away despite the suffering that brought her to Meskine. She had a particularly stubborn infection in the bone of her hip that was still being treated after a few months, trying to get it under control. When the infection was finally resolved, it left some destruction behind in the hip joint and pelvis, which meant that Jamilla had much-reduced joint mobility and a limp, but at least she could still walk and was well again. On her second visit to the hospital, one of the visiting doctors introduced Lee to Jamilla as it became apparent that Jamilla would be staying around for a while longer and could do with a friend who spoke Fulfulde.

This time she had come because she was seven months pregnant and, due to the lack of mobility around her pelvic area, it was advised that she deliver her first child where she could get medical help, just in case she needed to have an operation to get the baby out. She was camping out with her mother in the hospital grounds, waiting for the time to arrive, as her father did not want her to have to travel to the hospital from the bush too near to her delivery date. They were surrounded by all the supplies they needed for the next few months: food, mats, bedding, cooking pots, wood for the fire, water containers and clothes, all piled neatly next to them under the hangar next to the wards. Patiently they sat and waited.

At the first introductions Lee was met with a huge welcome and torrent of rapid Fulfulde as Jamilla was overjoyed to meet a foreigner who could understand her language. The warmth and love coming from this young woman to Lee was overwhelming as they exchanged greetings and held each other's hands; this was the friendliest Pullo Lee had ever met, for sure!

As Jamilla and her mother played the waiting game at the hospital, they made friends with all the other caregivers around them. The temporary community under the hangar became their world for the next couple of months. Every day Lee would stop by to chat with the group gathered around Jamilla, exchanging the all-important greetings and getting news updates of everyone's sick relatives. Lee would strain to understand as they fired their lightning speed Fulfulde at her. She, in turn, would relay some news about herself: mother of three, only ever had one husband, never had a co-wife, follower of Jesus, never milked a cow. To Jamilla this was all so fascinating as she had never been able to sit down and chat to a white woman in this manner before. At times there were misunderstandings as Lee tried to find the right words to express herself in Fulfulde, but it didn't really matter as there was such ease and love between them.

After a few meetings like this, Lee offered Jamilla and her new friends the *Jesus* film to watch. The group was really keen and all gathered around the small portable screen for several consecutive nights to view the film. Lee then asked one of the ladies if she understood why Jesus had died on the cross, and her answer was rather surprising. She responded, 'Jesus had to die because he turned over all the tables and stalls in the marketplace and everyone was angry at him!' It was obvious that, although these women had seen the film several times in their language, they were not listening to the words with understanding – hearing and listening were not the same thing.

As Jamilla watched the *Jesus* film over and over again in the evenings, Lee was perceiving that she was taking it in more and more each time, unlike her neighbours. Every day as Lee visited she would ask Jamilla, 'Did you enjoy the film again?' and she always responded, 'This man Jesus Christ, I like Jesus Christ!' Something was beginning to touch Jamilla's heart, so Lee went ahead and attempted to share the gospel in her stumbling Fulfulde. As she battled her way through the complicated grammar and vocabulary, she sensed that the Holy Spirit was taking over, enabling Jamilla to grasp the meaning of Jesus' death and resurrection. When Lee had finished, she asked Jamilla if she had understood and what she thought about it all. Jamilla had no doubts and immediately answered, 'I want Jesus. I want to follow him too!' There and then, Lee was able to lead her friend into the first day of the rest of her life as Jamilla prayed, asking Jesus to become her Lord.

Despite being really busy with various projects at the hospital, Lee continued to find time to meet with Jamilla every day, teaching her what it meant to be a disciple of Jesus. The challenges of language for Lee and illiteracy for Jamilla meant it was rather slow progress, but the joy of seeing Jamilla learn more and more about Jesus made the effort worthwhile. All the time as Jamilla was growing as a new creation in Christ,[2] her baby was getting ready to be born; finally, delivery day arrived.

Lee was not notified when Jamilla's labour first began during the evening. It turned into a very difficult night for Jamilla as she suffered with incredible pain; her pelvis was just too crooked and small for the baby to descend. The damage from her previously infected hip was now creating new problems for her and her baby as there was not enough space. At 5:30 a.m. the maternity nurse finally called Lee, explaining that her friend was in late-stage labour. Lee immediately ran up to the delivery room on the maternity ward to find Jamilla suffering with pain and exhaustion. Dr Martin, a surgeon from Germany, came in to examine her and concluded that a vaginal delivery was not going to be possible due to the lack of pelvic mobility. They would have to do a Caesarian section.

This was not what Jamilla wanted to hear at all. In an effort to reassure her, Lee explained that she would go to surgery with her, but first had to return home to inform her husband what was going on as she had suddenly disappeared from the house. Before she left, Lee told Jamilla that they needed to ask Jesus to help get this baby out somehow, so they quickly prayed, asking for a miracle. Lee squeezed Jamilla's hand that was tightly gripping hers, explaining that God was with her and not to be afraid. Lee then hurried out of the ward to her home, which was about 100 metres away, to tell Scott what was going on. As she was doing this the phone rang in her house. Picking it up, Lee heard the nurse on the other end shouting, '*Madame, le bébé est là, le bébé est là!*' – 'the baby is here! He explained that one minute after Lee left, the baby was born vaginally and was healthy and perfect; no surgery was needed after all! When Dr Martin returned to the maternity unit and heard what had happened, he announced, 'I have no doubt that the Lord intervened here!' Jamilla had experienced her first miracle with her first-born child, and from that day she knew that there was power in the name of Jesus.

Jamilla, her new son and her mother stayed at the hospital for another month until the family came to bring them home to their camp in the bush. Lee had continued visiting them each day, helping Jamilla to learn more about what it meant to be a follower of Jesus, but the day came when she had to let her dear friend go and trust the Holy Spirit to teach her how to stay close to Jesus. Jamilla could not read, so Lee could not give her a Bible; she had no phone, so Lee could not download an audio Bible for her to listen to; at that time we did not have any solar-charged devices to listen to the audio Bible either. The only thing Lee could do was to pray and trust the Holy Spirit to do the rest.

Lee didn't see Jamilla for quite some time after that. In the following years, though, Jamilla returned to the hospital to have two more children; each time God did the miracle of getting those babies out without the need for surgery. One time she made the long, hard journey just to ask Scott and Lee to pray for her as they were facing a huge crisis as a family. It was actually her mother who encouraged Jamilla to make the journey. She told her daughter that since they were facing a very difficult situation, she must go to *Baaba* and *Daada* Aisatou[3] (Scott and Lee) and ask them to pray, stressing to Jamilla, 'We have already seen how God answers their prayers; remember how easy it was for your children to be born!' Jamilla's mother never embraced Christ, as far as Lee knew, but she did see how praying in Jesus' name was powerful.

Scott attempted to explain to Jamilla that she didn't have to make that long journey to ask them to pray for her because she now had Jesus in her life, therefore had direct access to God because of what Jesus had done for her. Jesus was now her mediator to God. It wasn't easy to know how much Jamilla understood, but it was clear that she knew that only Jesus could help her. After chatting together some more about life with Jesus and praying together, Jamilla went back home to her people, reassuring her mother that *Baaba* and *Daada* Aisatou had prayed that the crisis would be resolved. Not long after, Lee received the phone call to say that all was well and that Jamilla and her family were again rejoicing that God had done a miracle and answered their prayers. Jamilla's assurance that Jesus was her rescuer was confirmed again.

During Jamilla's previous visit to Meskine, Lee had expressed her own desire to visit her camp to see how her family do life together. When the opportunity presented itself, she and Scott, along with another Pullo believer, began their journey to find Jamilla and her family. Being from the nomadic tradition, they were not of the habit of staying in one place for very long, so finding their camp became quite an adventure. After five hours of driving in the bush, asking one person after another along the way, they finally found them, much to Jamilla's surprise as she had no idea that they would actually come. The whole clan soon gathered to welcome the visitors as they had all heard about *Baaba* and *Daada* Aisatou from Meskine.

Jamilla's camp was typical of nomadic Fulbe, also known as Mbororo, out in the bush and away from other villages. It was a collection of domed huts made out of branches and grass, not high enough to stand up in but wide enough to spread out a mat and lie down. One part of the camp was kept for the cattle, with the central rope on the ground marking it out as the special area. The few trees that were around had bundles of clothes and calabashes with various contents balanced among the branches. And that was about it – no bathrooms, no extra shade, no hint of the modern world anywhere. The three visitors were offered Jamilla's father's 'welcoming hut' to sleep in, which also had thousands of flies and a few bats on hand to add to the welcoming committee. A ram was slaughtered that first evening to honour them, and fresh cow's milk was served three times each day.

The visit coincided with the task of building a new hut for one of Jamilla's relatives, so Lee was invited to join in the fun as the women were in charge of the building projects, while the men were out shepherding the massive herd of cows. Within one day the ladies had expertly hand-crafted a sturdy home with the bed frame being the foundational piece. This was house-building Mbororo style.

Knowing that the *Jesus* film has made such an impact on Jamilla and enabled her to respond to the gospel, Scott decided to offer it to the rest of her family too. He had come equipped with a portable DVD-player already charged, and the family were immediately intrigued to know what they were about to see. They willingly gathered under the stars to watch and listen to a story they had never heard of before. It was a long shot, but Scott thought it was worth a try to see if anyone else was interested in the gospel. There was some receptivity but, really, it just didn't make much sense to them after one viewing. Here were a couple of foreigners bringing their foreign story; it was entertaining but they didn't quite make the connection that they were also implicated in the story. Scott spoke with a few of the men the next day to find out what they thought of the film, but their culture of guarding their thoughts and emotions, and apprehension kept them from being vulnerable. It might have been different if the visitors had been able to stay with Jamilla's family for a more extended time, as trust could have been built up. Even so, some seeds of the gospel had been planted and it gave Jamilla a platform to work from as she shared with the rest of her family her experiences of Jesus in her own life.

For some reason, Jamilla had been the one God had chosen from among her clan to meet Jesus first, so that she could then be a witness to the power of Jesus to those who had not yet heard. Why would God choose a little woman like this with no apparent influence? For sure she was strong; her incredible patience through physical suffering had proven this. She was certainly a Pullo through and through; her manner of talking, dressing, behaving all pointed to this without a shred of doubt. But she was illiterate and slow to grasp new information; surely this was not the person who could make the biggest impact for the sake of Jesus – or was she? Actually, the childlike response that Jamilla had towards Jesus is exactly what God is looking for. Jesus himself declared, 'Truly I tell you, anyone who will not receive the kingdom of God like a little child will never enter it' (Luke 18:17). The way Jamilla ran to Jesus when she first heard about him, the way she learned to love him and brought all her problems and struggles to him as a child does with its father, led her into an experience of the power of Jesus and answers to prayer that few of us can boast about. A childlike heart leading to a childlike faith can be an incredibly powerful combination when it's all about Jesus.

Our experience in inviting Fulbe and other Muslims to follow Jesus has not always been so easy as it was with Jamilla though. A cloud of fear and unbelief seemed to be a permanent fixture over many that blocked out the warmth and light that Jesus longed to shine into their lives. How was this cloud ever to be blown away?

11

Faith, Fear and Fruitfulness

'My people don't want to know Jesus! Their heads are too hard to even think about wanting him! The worst thing they could imagine is to become a follower of Jesus! I'm the only one who wants to follow him; all the others don't understand and they are never going to listen to me!'

As I listened to my new sister in Christ venting at me, it felt like another defeat. It seemed that whenever our team ventured to encourage the new Fulbe followers of Jesus to pray for their people and seek for opportunities to share the good news of Jesus with others, their initial thoughts were, 'It's impossible.' Jesus' final command to his disciples was, frankly, beginning to feel rather like an impossible task to us too. But why would Jesus command us to do something if it was impossible? There had to be a way for more Fulbe to discover Jesus.

Grappling with the Faith of the Fulbe

'Therefore go and make disciples of all nations, baptising them in the name of the Father and of the Son and of the Holy Spirit, and teaching them to obey everything I have commanded you' (Matt. 28:19–20). Missionaries all over the world have meditated on these words of Jesus repeatedly. These words have in fact changed the course of their lives, turned their world upside down, thrown them into cultural confusion and linguistic gymnastics, caused them to do things they had never thought necessary or even possible! How could these few words have such a dramatic effect? And how could these few words be so complicated and difficult to obey? These are the questions that I have often pondered, and I have no doubt that my team-mates in Meskine have done the same at some point.

The very existence of Meskine Hospital is based on the hope and intention of being obedient to Jesus' final command. MCWA was birthed out of a calling to go and make disciples of Jesus among the Fulbe and Fulfulde-speaking Muslims, who were known to be unreached with the gospel. When the MCWA team arrived in Cameroon we found a well-established church originating from the non-Muslim minority people groups of the region, but they were not engaging their Muslim neighbours with the gospel in a very fruitful or effective manner. MCWA was part of a new wave of missionaries in the 1980s and 1990s to the Muslims of northern and sub-Saharan Africa, and wanted to contribute to a change by establishing a medical work that could be used as a platform from which to make disciples. Go. Build a hospital. Tell people about Jesus. Make disciples. We wanted to be obedient to Jesus and do just this, but the challenge we faced felt rather like climbing Mount Everest without oxygen.

As a team of novices in bringing the gospel of Jesus to Muslims, we depended on the experience of others in order to be effective, so we paid attention to what other missionaries were doing in similar cultures around the world.[1] We began by pursuing an approach that was known as 'friendship evangelism'. This refers to the vehicle of friendship and building a relationship in order to 'get to the gospel' in conversation and earn the right to talk about Jesus with your Muslim friend. Living among the people in the neighbourhoods and pursuing contacts made when people had been hospitalized led to much time being invested in building deeper friendships, with the goal of being able to talk about our hope in Jesus one day. Not surprisingly, we found that this method led to us having lots of friends, very dear ones whom we loved but, frustratingly, hardly any of them wanted to know Jesus for themselves. The heartache of the beloved friend rejecting the beloved Saviour never goes away. Having invested months, even years of time in a friendship only to discover that it was simply that, just a friendship, became rather discouraging.

It was more than obvious at the beginning that, if we were going to get into deep spiritual conversations with our friends, we had to work hard at acquiring the difficult Fulfulde language; to some this was a delight and to others it was a drudgery. Just knowing French was not going to be enough in order to make deeper relationships with people, as Fulfulde was generally the heart language, and often only language, of most Muslims in the area. After about a year of intentional study, most of us long-term team members made enough progress in the language to feel as though we had at least got a decent foundation and were no longer completely lost in a conversation. Realistically, though, it was obvious that this language would never be conquered and that there would always be new things to learn. It was like peeling an onion with endless layers; it made you cry, but you knew that it would make life taste better in the end! Along with language acquisition came a deeper understanding of the Fulbe culture and mindset, which we discovered was deeply rooted in their Muslim faith.

In the early years, Scott spent hours talking to men in the village, gathered under the neem trees, longing to find an open heart that wanted to hear more about Jesus and the gospel; but it became a slow and laborious task. Frances, and others of us who joined the team later, spent hours visiting women in their homes seeking to find an opening in the conversation that would lead to Jesus. It became clear to us that there was a wall of indoctrination that apparently had to be penetrated before a heart could be opened to listen to the gospel. A mind and heart that has been taught a faith that is not based on the love of God, but rather on one's own efforts to please God, leads to a blindness and deafness to the message of grace that is embodied in Jesus Christ. Not only this, but we discovered that Muslims have been taught so many historically and biblically incorrect things about the Bible and Jesus that our message seemed like a foreign language to them.[2] Countless times in conversations, our efforts were met with the same comments from our friends:

'The Bible has been corrupted so you can't trust anything in it, therefore you should not read it.'

'The prophet Jesus did not really die on the cross, but ascended straight to heaven without dying.'

'When the prophet Jesus returns to earth, he will become a Muslim, marry and have children.'

'The prophet Jesus told his disciples that the prophet Mohammad would come after him and that he would be the final prophet.'

And so it went on. Day after day, visit after visit, we would find ourselves having the same conversations, which would often lead to debate, which in turn would lead to frustration on both sides of the discussion. Friendship evangelism was very hard work and the rewards were few and far between.

It became abundantly clear to us that the most important thing was for Muslims to have the opportunity to engage with the Bible for themselves. How were they ever going to grasp an alternative view of Jesus if they never got to engage with the evidence? Whether it be paper booklets, videos, pictures, audio cassettes, micro-SD memory cards or phone apps, being able to access the word of God for themselves was the most effective means of getting the message across, or at least a good starting point. Global Recordings Network[3] has been incredibly helpful for many years in providing resources to give people access to the Bible in their own language, and we have been very grateful recipients of many of their devices. Ones that proved to be very popular for a time were the hand-wound and solar-charged devices, as finally people could listen to the Bible without having to replace batteries all the time! In later years, with the mobile phone explosion, it became all about using micro-SD memory cards, phone apps and websites. Whatever form it takes, nothing beats getting people to experience God's word for themselves, and lack of literacy need not be a barrier.

When David and Patsy Alfors joined our team in 2004 from ReachGlobal, they brought with them a wealth of experience from working in the Democratic Republic of Congo and CAR. Their desire to work among the Fulbe led them to Meskine; little did they know that we had been asking God to send more workers to focus on the disciple-making side of our ministry. We specifically asked God for people who could speak French and Fulfulde (their knowledge of Lingala and Arabic were added bonuses) and people with church-planting experience. David and Patsy were a perfect fit for us. Being expert doughnut and ice-cream makers and extremely generous hosts have ensured that they are indispensable and have attained legendary status on our team! David's ability to fix just about anything, love of technology and teaching skills with language learning have been an incredible contribution. Patsy's steady perseverance in sowing the seeds of the gospel among the women in Meskine and beyond has been remarkable. When they first came, Patsy brought a set of pictures that could be used in Bible story-telling which proved to be a huge hit, especially among the women in the village. It didn't take long for the rest of us to try it out at the hospital and in the village too. Having a picture really helped illiterate people to focus and recall the story, so in this way, many heard the salvation story from creation to Christ. At one point Patsy reported that she was regularly visiting over fifty women in Meskine to share Bible stories with, some of whom came to faith in Jesus.

When there was an opening to talk about the gospel with Fulbe and other Muslims, it often felt like a mini-miracle and a breath of fresh air. A curious question, a comment, a sense of searching in the conversation, a positive response to prayer – these things became cues and prompts to press further to find out if this person was searching for Jesus. Some people had been searching for a long time and when they finally had an opportunity to learn from the Bible themselves it made sense to them. Others had experienced dreams that nudged them to want to know more about Jesus, or were looking for assurance of forgiveness of sin that they could not find in Islam. Still others responded to the power of healing prayer in Jesus' name. It was therefore becoming evident that it is not impossible for Fulbe and Muslims to come to faith in Jesus Christ. When there is a searching, hungry heart for truth, for hope, for assurance of what lies after death and an encounter with the power and person of Jesus, then the walls of the Muslim faith come tumbling down.

When Fear Takes Over

Bakka was one of those whose heart was ready to respond. During the early days of hospital construction there were a few Muslims working as labourers in the crew and one of these men was drawn to the early morning gatherings before work began, where the team committed the day into God's hands. As the Christian workers gathered under a tree to pray and worship God, Bakka would be on the periphery but listening to all that was going on. After a little while he approached a visiting volunteer from the UK and asked if she had anything from the Bible that he could read, as curiosity had taken hold of him. As Scott had already started to make good progress with Fulfulde, it was suggested that Bakka talk to him, as they would be able to communicate more deeply. Scott gave Bakka some tracts and Bible portions in Fulfulde and found that he could read quite well. At that point Bakka was not asking any specific questions about the Bible or Jesus, but when he read a short tract explaining why Jesus had to die on the cross his heart and mind were opened to the gospel. He was so touched by the tract that he carried it around everywhere with him in his pocket for weeks afterwards, reading it over and over.

It wasn't long before Scott and Bakka began to read through Luke's Gospel together. When they got to Luke 9, Scott asked Bakka the same question that Jesus asked his disciples: 'Bakka, who do you say Jesus is?'

Bakka took a long pause and thought about his answer, finally replying, 'Jesus is the Messiah and he is the greatest prophet.'

By this point Bakka had already seen the *Jesus* film and when it came to the crucifixion scene, he had been greatly moved that

Jesus would go through that agony for the sake of others. Scott now took the time to explain the gospel more clearly to Bakka so he could understand why the Messiah is our Saviour and not just a prophet. That day, Bakka confessed that he believed Jesus to be his Saviour and wanted to follow him. After they had prayed together, Bakka lifted his head and gazed at Scott with a very solemn expression on his face, announcing, 'You know what's going to happen now, don't you? I'm going to have serious problems with my people when I tell them I want to follow Jesus.' Bakka was expressing a deep-seated fear that we would come to see in many other Fulbe who accepted Christ. It was a very genuine fear of their people and their community that their new faith in Christ would lead them into isolation, and even violence. The fact that Cameroon governs with freedom of religion made little impact on the Muslim communities as they pursued their own laws and agendas.

For the first time, Scott had to have the difficult conversation with a new follower of Jesus that persecution was inevitable but that there were ways to be wise in communicating their new faith with loved ones. Bakka had already received threats and intimidation from people in the village who knew he had been visiting Scott regularly, and Bakka had already become fearful of the consequences of what following Jesus openly would bring. In discipling Bakka, Scott was to discover the harmful consequences that being bound by fear of others brings. Fear inhibits spiritual growth in every way and does not lead to the abundant life that Jesus promised. Scott encouraged Bakka to take his time in conveying the truths of the gospel to those around him, but this exhortation was 'lost in translation' and rather interpreted as 'be careful', which in turn sowed more seeds of fear. Over the years all of us have had the same struggles with people we have been discipling; fear of other people quenches the life-giving work of the Holy Spirit in the new follower of Christ.

Bakka is still a believer in Jesus all these years later, still reads his Bible and meets with a few other brothers in Christ from time to time. However, his fear of persecution has caused him to remain a rather secret believer, which consequently means he has not had the privilege of leading others to Christ. We often saw this situation repeated among other Fulbe believers. They wanted Jesus for themselves but fear of persecution and rejection by their community prevented them from sharing the good news with others. They had a big secret and were essentially afraid of the consequences from their family and community if it was found out. The thought of becoming socially isolated was too painful, and as most of them were already living on the poverty line, it almost seemed suicidal to them to risk losing their whole support network. As we discipled them, we too did not encourage them to come out in the open with their new faith in Christ immediately, unless they wanted to. Rather, we encouraged them to carry on living among their people, praying for them and asking God to show them how to be salt and light[4] where they were, with the aim of being able to introduce the rest of their family to Jesus one day. Retrospectively, we realized that we were in fact raising our spiritual children under a cloud of fear, which hindered their spiritual growth, and in turn tended to stifle the work of the Holy Spirit in their lives.

Despite this, some of these 'secret believers' began to meet together in small groups of men and women each week, and from time to time they would come together. On other occasions, Fulbe believers who lived further away were invited to come to a larger gathering, so the numbers could swell to twenty or thirty people. These were happy occasions with a real sense that progress was being made towards planting a 'Fulbe church'. Reading the Bible and praying together, eating together, hearing one another's stories and struggles, supporting each other as they were baptized and sharing the Lord's Supper together were all major steps forward as they journeyed with Jesus. But the fact that these Fulbe believers were not passing on what they were learning about Jesus was troubling to us. How were the rest of the Fulbe people going to hear about Jesus if it was left up to us missionaries to do it? We longed and prayed for God to show us what the next step should be.

Moving from Fear to Fruitfulness

In 2007 Scott and I, and later Jacqueline, attended some training seminars being held in N'Djamena, Chad. We had been invited to come and hear a man from the USA who had experience working among Muslims elsewhere. We didn't quite know what the seminars were going to be about, but because they were strongly recommended, we thought we should go and investigate. What we heard over the next couple of days blew our strategy and minds apart. This experienced missionary of many years was advocating a change of direction in ministry strategy that began to resonate with our team.

He explained that when most of the people he had been discipling were persecuted and killed, it led him to completely start again, looking at the gospels and Jesus' methods of disciple-making to see how he could change his own approach. Out of his studies and further application, along with other missionaries following similar lines of thought, the global conversation among church planters working in Muslim situations was beginning to shift from 'friendship evangelism' to disciple-making movements (DMM). Basically, from relooking at the gospels and studying Jesus' own strategy, which led to a disciple-making movement that can be seen unfolding in the book of Acts, our eyes were opened to see what could be possible if we changed the way we approached ministry. Jesus modelled and taught his disciples to engage people with the message of the gospel as a priority and not invest extended time in people who were not receptive, nor willing to share with others.[5]

It was clear that being a 'secret believer' had no place in this way of life. Sharing the gospel with your people, and other lost people around you, was a basic mark of being a follower of Jesus. Obedience to Jesus' commands was foundational, and 'following and fishing' were the new way of life he was expecting – follow Jesus as Lord and be fishers of men (Mark 1:17). Investing time in people who especially had this commitment was bound to be the most fruitful direction to follow long-term in order to make other disciples of Jesus. This began a season of radical reorientation in ministry strategy for our team. In the months that followed we spent much time in research, prayer, self-examination and discussion with others who had more experience than ourselves with this strategy. A visit from a Fulbe brother in Christ from Burkina Faso encouraged us further to make intentional changes, as he himself had made with his team, in order to see the Fulbe in Cameroon coming to Christ with real transformation and the numbers we longed for.

The concept of 'friendship evangelism' also no longer seemed adequate to what we were wanting to do. We found that taking years to build friendships and deep relationships with people before sharing the gospel had led to only a few of our friends opening their hearts to Jesus. Love and friendship alone were not being very fruitful as far as making disciples of Jesus was concerned; we recognized the need to 'get to the point' of the gospel earlier on in our conversations with our friends. Consequently, we took a change of direction by becoming more intentional in sharing the gospel as soon as possible with contacts and then encouraging those who were listening to go on and share it with their families and friends, even if they had not come to faith in Christ themselves yet. 'What you have learned today about God, who are you going to share it with now?' became one of our parting questions each time. This more direct approach did not, however, mean that we stopped being friends with people or stopped being generous with the love of Christ. It simply meant that we became more focused in our conversations with new friends and old alike.

We also altered the way we looked at the Bible with contacts who wanted to know more. Rather than teaching or 'storying', which inevitably meant we were doing most of the talking, we sought to help people discover for themselves what the Bible was saying through simple methods, using inductive questions to guide discussion. Trusting the Holy Spirit to do what Jesus said he would do was the incentive – teach, convict, counsel, and guide into truth.[6]

Mamadou came into our lives around the time that we were learning these new ways, and was one who faced up to his fears and started to share his new-found faith in Jesus with his family. He found himself at our hospital for several weeks, having had some complicated and life-altering surgery. Danny first met Mamadou during the prayer round one evening, leading to more conversations which opened the way for him to come to faith in Christ. On follow-up visits to his home village, Mamadou reported that he had been sharing with his family what he had been learning, but they initially reacted in a very hostile manner, being very unhappy with his decision to follow

Jesus. His mother even tried to poison him on three different occasions in an effort to bring him back to Islam, but when this failed to have the effect she desired, she realized that she was fighting a losing battle. In time, Mamadou's wife began to listen to the gospel, as did a small group of his friends in the neighbourhood. Mamadou was greatly encouraged to press on in sharing his faith when another believer from a Muslim background started to visit him regularly to read the Bible with him. This brief example illustrates that in stepping out and sharing his faith, despite initial hostility from his family, Mamadou experienced the power of God and the joy of sharing Jesus with others that he never would have known if he had remained a 'secret believer'.

One of the most encouraging transformations we have witnessed from fear to fruitfulness in a follower of Jesus who has left Islam is a man called Saali. For several years Saali wavered between feast and famine when it came to pursuing Jesus. At times he came regularly for Bible studies and had lots of questions, then weeks and months would pass before he turned up again wanting to know more. His typical, indirect way of communicating and extreme politeness made it difficult for us to know what was going on in his thoughts, but one thing was for certain, he was curious about Jesus and the Bible.

After many years of research and ponderings, Saali finally came to faith in Jesus as his Lord. After this huge step, his deep joy in reading the Bible was tangible whenever he came to visit. A broad smile was often displayed on his face as he explained the new thing he had learned from the Bible that week. Saali had been a teacher of the Qur'an, so was used to sitting down with people to discuss deep spiritual things, but his life was now turned upside down as he absorbed all these new wonderful truths from the Bible. He was not, however, ready to share what he was learning with others, as he knew there would be opposition that would make his life very difficult. It took many months for him to build up the courage to engage his friends in conversation about Jesus, but he devised ways, often using the Qur'an, to grab their attention or raise a question. He invited some of his friends to read the Bible with him and began to share about Jesus with his family.

As word got out that Saali was reading the Bible, his neighbours started to shun him, stopped eating with him and called him a dirty pagan for leaving Islam. There were others in the village, though, who were searching for the truth about Jesus or who had questions of faith. They sought out Saali and came to him with their questions; consequently, he has had the wonderful privilege of leading some of them to faith in Christ. He now particularly enjoys visiting other Fulbe believers to encourage them to persevere and not give up following Christ and longs to see more of his people worshipping Jesus one day.

Mission Accomplished?

It is difficult to measure at this point in our story how far along we are in seeing a movement of Fulbe disciples making other Fulbe disciples in community. When will the final vision of MCWA be accomplished? An important measurement that is frequently used in DMM circles to gauge whether the goal of a disciple-making movement is being accomplished is the achievement of fourth-generation disciples.[7] This is what dreams are made of in the disciple-maker's world, and in many places, it is becoming a reality.

We are still working towards this goal, with faith that God will accomplish it. What can be said at this stage is that we are seeing Fulbe and other Fulfulde-speaking Muslims coming to faith in Christ in increasing numbers. Some of these disciples are beginning to lead some of their people to Christ and making other disciples. In some locations there are family groups and communities who are now following Jesus together. Children of Fulbe are now being born to parents who call themselves *Masiihinko 'en*, 'followers of the Messiah'. These children will not grow up reciting the Qur'an or learning to practise the five-times-a-day prayers of Islam as their parents did, but will grow up knowing about Jesus Christ and learning from the Bible. There are increasing gatherings of Fulbe believers meeting in homes and other locations. With the production in 2018 of the whole Bible in Arabic-script Fulfulde (known as *Ajamiya*), there is now a Bible that the Fulbe can call their own, that they are keen to read and distribute.

What is being seen, also by others who have been working among the Fulbe for many years, are hopeful signs that the Fulbe church is emerging and alive. MCWA continues to ask the question, 'What is it going to take for the whole Fulbe nation and other Muslim peoples of Cameroon to hear the gospel and have an opportunity to respond?' It is still a daunting task, but not as daunting as it was twenty-five years ago. It seems that this is the time in history when the Fulbe are beginning to respond to Jesus in greater numbers than have been seen before, which is reflective of what God is doing in the wider Muslim world.[8]

For MCWA, it will take continued commitment and refocusing to train, equip and encourage Fulbe believers and other Cameroonian Christians, so that they can be intentional in getting the good news of Jesus out to those who have yet to hear. It will take prayer and more prayer. It will take leadership training and development. It will take time. It will take courage. As far as MCWA is concerned, there is still work to be done, and there will continue to be intention and commitment to seeing the task finished. We know we serve the God of whom it is said, 'all things are possible' (Matt. 19:26). With the love of the heavenly Father, the grace of the Lord Jesus Christ and the fellowship of the Holy Spirit, the Fulbe church will grow and take its place in the worldwide body of Christ.

As we strive towards this end, we cannot ignore the reality of persecution that Fulbe and other followers of Jesus from a Muslim background face. As I write this, my heart is heavy as one of our Fulbe brothers grieves for the death of his 11-year-old son who was attacked by other youths and died from his injuries. The only reason for this brutal attack was that this boy's father is now a follower of Jesus. Some members of the body of Christ pay a high and painful price for their faith. There is one woman who has especially taught me what it means to suffer for him.

12

Singing Her Own Song

Adda knows her own mind and is not afraid to say so. 'Feisty' comes to mind when trying to describe her, along with confident, brave, beautiful, creative, intelligent, resilient and infuriating. This young woman came crashing into our world after her own was turned upside down by a road accident. I found her at our hospital when I returned to Cameroon as a long-termer, in November 2000. She had already been with us for a few months, and this was after spending six months at other hospitals nearby. Adda was now strung up on femoral traction in another effort to treat her shattered leg. Dr Bert and his team were ready to try anything to get this leg to heal, but it was proving to be very challenging.

What had been meant to be a milestone day of achievement earlier in the year had turned into a terrible nightmare. Adda had been on the back of a motorcycle taxi, on her way to take her exams for the baccalaureate, which is the final hurdle in leaving school. In a few seconds her dreams were destroyed as a careless driver rammed into the motorcycle Adda was on, crushing her leg and leaving her with a terrible fracture in her thigh and multiple other injuries. This led to months of hospital care, unsuccessful surgeries, repeated infections, painful wound dressings and endless antibiotics. After six months and no obvious improvement with the fracture, she came to our hospital to see if we had anything else to offer. It was to become another long stretch of hospitalization of several months before she was finally able to go home.

During this time I got to know Adda well, as did many others on the team and staff. She loved to have people around her, and being bed-bound by the traction meant having others sitting with her was her only option for social interaction. These were the days before mobile phones had become prolific and face-to-face conversation was still the norm. Adda was good at gathering people around her, as her love of conversation was a magnet to many. But something was missing. Where were her family? Her friends? Her neighbours? True, her mother was always there, faithfully taking care of her daughter, but it didn't take me long to realize that Adda had become isolated from her community.

Since a young age, Adda had been asking questions about God and the religion she had grown up in. Her grandfather had been a churchgoer as a young man, but when the first president of Cameroon, who was a Muslim, took office, it became more beneficial for men in business and public roles to be Muslim too. Positions of influence and leadership were generally given to those of 'like mind' with the president, so Adda's grandfather converted to Islam, along with many others. Thus, he raised his family in Islam and that is how Adda found herself growing up as a Muslim.

Her parents did not have a happy marriage, as her father drank too much alcohol for the home to be peaceful, but Adda grew up next to a Christian family who loved her and welcomed her into their home whenever she wanted to be there. In this caring, calm environment that was so different to her own home, this family became the aroma of Jesus to this rather neglected girl; they began to help Adda understand what was so special about Jesus. What she learned with this family stayed with her as she grew into a woman, and ultimately changed her life forever.

Adda came from a family that valued education, so she was able to get a level of schooling that was still uncommon for girls in the region. She had an aptitude for learning and developed a quizzical and questioning mind, never taking anything as truth until she had researched it for herself, coming to a reasoned conclusion. This approach was very much in contrast to the majority of the women around her, especially those who were Muslims. The general cultural rule for them was not to question anything but to accept what you have been told by those who deemed themselves to know more than you. This did not sit comfortably with Adda, so she continued to question what Islam offered her, and began to read the Bible to learn more about Jesus. She had school friends who were followers of Jesus and she could see that their lives were so different to hers; there was something they had that she wanted. The more she discovered, the more she was drawn to Jesus himself, and at some point in her mid-teens her heart had chosen to believe that Jesus was her Saviour and her Lord. This was a quiet realization rather than a public declaration; Adda herself probably would not have called herself a 'Christian' at that point because the title did not hold meaning for her. She kept it all in her heart until she found herself trapped in a hospital bed.

Not long after the accident, Adda's fiancé stopped visiting her. I guess he saw that his future bride was not going to make a quick or good recovery, and he didn't want to wait for her. After six months in hospital her family also started to get twitchy and tired of paying the expensive hospital bills, thinking she should just come home and take whatever God had planned for her life. But there was a Catholic priest who befriended Adda while she was in hospital in Maroua. He took the time to talk to her, to see her pain, to understand her difficult situation and even to start helping pay her medical bills. He also answered her many questions about Jesus. Finally, she found that she couldn't keep her faith in Christ a secret from her family any more.

By the time Adda came to our hospital, her family and friends realized that she was no longer 'theirs', that she had chosen to bring shame on them by rejecting Islam and turning to Jesus. This was why the only visitors to her bedside were hospital employees, missionaries and other Christians. Her mother could not leave her, for a mother's love is as strong as death, but I could see the pain and bewilderment on her face, as if to say, 'Why has my daughter walked away from us and brought shame on us in this way?' In the mind of a Muslim, the worst thing that anyone could do is to turn away from Islam. The Qur'an[1] teaches that anyone who does this will be doomed to face God's wrath. Some teachings of the Hadith[2] go further, saying that the punishment for such apostasy is death and this is indeed the type of justice that is meted out to those who turn to Christ in some parts of the world today. It is little wonder, then, that Adda's mother and wider family were so distressed by her decision to follow Christ.

Despite being physically trapped in her bed, the reality was in fact the opposite to Adda in other ways. She was experiencing a liberation in finally being able to talk to people openly about her faith in Jesus. She devoured her Bible, often reading it aloud for all to hear. Her heart was still in turmoil because of her leg's refusal to heal and all that she had lost since the accident, but she was also like a newborn baby that grows incredibly fast. Her faith was galloping along as she asked questions, discussed, prayed, cried and praised all at the same time. The future for her was so uncertain in a practical sense. What was she going to do now? Would she even be able to walk? Will she ever be married? What will her family do to her? Yet, in the midst of all these swirling thoughts, Adda knew that she had an anchor that would hold her fast in the coming turbulent days.

Finally, after several months of medical treatment and physiotherapy, the day came for her to leave hospital. She was now walking on crutches but still not able to bear weight on her fragile leg, as the infection had prevented new bone growth. She left us with a cloud of uncertainty hanging over her, heading off to stay at her grandfather's house. She knew it was going to be tough, but she didn't expect what she found.

The day she arrived home her family had all come together for a meeting, not to welcome her but to face the shame that Adda had brought on them, once and for all. It was plainly told to Adda that either she renounce Christ and return to Islam or she was no longer a part of this family and must leave immediately. Adda's heart was broken again. She knew she could not leave Jesus, as the salvation of her soul was more precious to her than anything else; how could she stop loving Jesus, the One who loved her more than anyone else had ever done? That day she had to choose to leave her family. She limped out of that house with her crutches and the one bag she could carry, out onto the street with no idea where she could go.

At that moment, God in his mercy brought along an evangelist from a local church who had got to know Adda, like so many others, while she was at our hospital. 'Adda, what are you doing out here? I thought you had gone home.' Then the whole story flowed out, along with her tears. Knowing that he couldn't leave his vulnerable friend in this predicament, he helped Adda onto the back of his motorcycle, placed her bag in front of him on the fuel tank and took her straight to a nearby church. The pastor graciously took her in and welcomed her; he had heard her story through the members of his church. Adda knew she was safe for now. Nobody knew at that moment how long she would be staying and, as days turned to weeks, the pastor gave her a one-roomed little house of her own on the church compound; that became her new home for many more months.

These were dark, sad, tumultuous days for Adda. I and others from Meskine visited her regularly and there were often tears and cries of lament. Her heart had been broken by the rejection of her family. Now she found herself in a completely new social circle and struggling to know how she could fit in. She was literally living in the grounds of a church, and to her family, this was enemy territory. They would never visit her here, even if she hadn't left Islam. During this season Adda was learning that her strength would come from Father God. Many times we would read something from the Psalms together that seemed to express just how she was feeling:

> How long, LORD? Will you forget me for ever? How long will you hide your face from me?
>
> How long must I wrestle with my thoughts and day after day have sorrow in my heart? How long will my enemy triumph over me?
>
> Look on me and answer, LORD my God. Give light to my eyes, or I will sleep in death,
>
> and my enemy will say 'I have overcome [her],' and my foes will rejoice when I fall.
>
> But I trust in your unfailing love; my heart rejoices in your salvation.
>
> I will sing the LORD's praise, for he has been good to me.
>
> Psalm 13:1–6

It was a constant battle for Adda in her heart and mind; the pain of loneliness and exclusion from her family, along with the severe physical difficulties of having a leg that didn't function as it should, fought alongside her joy in salvation and following Jesus Christ openly.

As time went on, Adda became stronger and more independent, to the extent that she felt confident to move off the church compound and into a rented home in the neighbourhood. Now being away from the protection of the church community, it wasn't long before she was visited by three hooded men late one evening. They chose a time when they knew she would be alone and they could get away undetected. They had come to threaten and intimidate her, saying, 'If you don't return to Islam then we will come back and slit your throat!' Having hurled some verbal insults at her, they left, warning her that they would be returning one day. Although Adda didn't recognize any of the men, she was convinced that her grandfather had arranged this as one more effort to scare her back into Islam. Sadly, this is a common tactic that only reveals the dark heart of a religious system that is broken and can only think of threats and violence as a way of keeping people under control. It did not work and only served to strengthen Adda's resolve to cling to Jesus, whatever the future might hold.

Her leg did finally heal, but in the end the movement of her knee was sacrificed for the healing of the bone. To this day Adda has a distinctive gait when she walks. A few years after the accident there was finally a court hearing, and the outcome was ruled in Adda's favour. It was announced that she should receive a sizeable financial compensation from the woman who had caused the accident, as she had the means to pay. However, as is often the case, this ruling was not carried out and justice was not done, as no steps were taken to ensure that Adda got what the judge had decreed. It was a frustrating mockery of justice instead. Adda was therefore denied an opportunity to achieve some kind of financial stability in her rocky life. Despite this huge setback, she was determined to gain some kind of financial independence. Her creative skills enabled her to earn a basic living by making colourful beaded jewellery to sell, but it was not an easy existence and loneliness was never far away.

She tried on several occasions, but was never really able to integrate into the established church, which is a common problem for those who leave Islam to follow Christ in Cameroon. It seems the established church finds it difficult to accept believers from a Muslim background and often doubts that these new brothers and sisters are genuine in their faith. This suspicion is regrettably based on past experiences when some individuals from a Muslim background have entered the church claiming to follow Jesus, but in fact are simply trying to make some financial gain from Christians. The truth was that Adda knew her Bible more deeply than many of the Christians I met in the Cameroonian church, but she was never accepted as 'one of the family'. Her baptism was a heart-wrenching example of this.

Adda had been planning this celebration for a while and was sure to invite many of her friends from Meskine. We were very happy to attend and celebrate with her and I was honoured to be asked by Adda to be one of those to pray for her after the baptism. The church was full, as the baptism would be part of the normal Sunday service. Adda was so sure that all the cost she had already paid to follow Jesus was worth it and wanted everyone to rejoice with her. She had seen the church modelling to her that when there was joy, there was singing. Muslims generally do not grow up singing and especially not as a way to worship and praise God, but Adda was trying to learn from the church activities going on around her. It turns out that she was not particularly gifted musically, but she so wanted to sing a song of praise to God on this special occasion of her baptism. A few friends had tried to talk her out of singing a solo, wondering if this was the best thing to do, knowing that she couldn't really hold a tune. But Adda was adamant that she wanted to bring this offering of praise to God.

So it was that after her baptism Adda stood in front of hundreds of people and sang her song of praise. This was the bravest woman I had seen in a long time. She could not find the 'official' melody of the song at all, and you would be mistaken for even realizing that she was singing. There were sniggers of stifled laughter around the church and even people saying out loud, 'What a shame she can't sing a note.' But Adda kept on going and brought that song of praise to her heavenly Father and to Jesus, who had given everything for her. At that moment my heart melted with love for this sister. There was nothing and no one who was going to stop Adda from celebrating the fact that she was now a child of God, a new creation; no pain, no injury, no insult, no intimidation, no isolation, no hardship, no fear. She became a giant of the faith in my eyes that day and remains so.

Adda has taught me that suffering for Jesus is always worth it because he is worthy; he has already paid the highest price and won for us the most precious gift of forgiveness and eternal life. The cost of following Jesus is never too high. As the years went on, Adda remained isolated from her family and paid the price for following Jesus every day. At the time of writing she is still not married; several men wanted to marry her, but in the end the arrangements were pulled apart by other members of the family or friends. She loved and served others readily with a generous heart, even taking on the educational responsibility of a young girl who had been abandoned by her father, despite not having a regular income of her own. She persevered in maintaining contact with her family even though they did little in reciprocation. She sought to honour her parents as much as she was allowed to. She never shied away from explaining her reason for choosing Christ over Islam and, since many came to ask her questions about this, she had plenty of opportunities.

In the end Adda could take the isolation from her family and from the church community no longer, deciding to move to a neighbouring country to start a new life there. I hope she has found freedom. I hope she has found a place to be herself and to be who God wants her to be. I hope she has found her place in the body of Christ, his church. I hope she is still singing her beautiful song of praise to the One she loves and the One who loves her without measure.

There were many traditions of her old life in Islam that Adda was overjoyed to become free from when she came to faith in Jesus. In many ways she truly felt Jesus had lifted the burden of empty religion from her shoulders. One month of the year especially reminded her of this new-found freedom and gave her cause to celebrate Christ every time it came around.

13

The Hardest Month of the Year

Ramadan, that huge annual marker of time in the Muslim world, is a lunar month of fasting from the daylight pleasures of eating and drinking, and anything else that is considered a pleasure such as TV, smoking, alcohol, sex, and general 'failings' such as lying or stealing. It is the month when every Muslim is expected to be on their very best behaviour in every way, a month to be as holy as you possibly can, a month to be as obedient as you possibly can to the demands and commands of the prophet Mohammad and all that Allah has dictated according to the Qur'an and Islamic traditions.

This time of year affects the rhythm of life in an all-encompassing way and it certainly made a huge impact on Meskine Hospital every year. As the month wore on, the number of patients coming would get lower and lower so that all the outpatient clinics were much quieter. Most patients decided to wait until after Ramadan to sort out their niggling health problems if they could do so, not only because of the physical inconvenience of coming to the hospital during that month but also because taking medication when you are meant to be fasting in daylight hours is a nuisance. Most people will do all they can to maintain the fast at the same time as everyone else, so even if you are mildly unwell you will still try to fast and follow tradition. Only if you are really sick will you come to the hospital during Ramadan. The knock-on effect of this was that the hospital income was always greatly reduced during this month, becoming expected as the facility grew. In some ways, it came as a relief to the staff after the busy times throughout the rest of the year; for one month of the year most workers felt they could go home on time at the end of the working day having finished their load.

As the time for Ramadan approaches each year there is a growing sense of people bracing themselves for the task of being the best Muslim and best version of themselves that they can be. Before it starts, relatives and friends go around visiting, or make phone calls, wishing their loved ones a 'pure Ramadan', with the collective sense that everyone is in this together and as a mutual encouragement to do your best. The women have the habit of cleaning their homes from top to bottom so it is as clean as possible before Ramadan gets going. There are a couple of explanations for this, depending on the degree of religious fervour. One reason given is that the home is another expression of one's holiness, and just as the body must be clean and pure to be acceptable to God, then so should our homes be, and even more so during Ramadan. A spotless, tidy, clean house is therefore a requirement for many families. Another more practical explanation for this mass cleaning is that during Ramadan women are so tired that they really don't have the energy to clean the house properly, so it's best to get it as clean as you can beforehand. All the furniture is scrubbed, the mattresses, the bedding, the rugs, all the pots and pans and everything else in the cabinets is brought outside and cleaned thoroughly. All the clothes are made clean in preparation.

Then there is the food shopping to be done, millet flour to be prepared, peanuts to be ground, essential supplies to be bought, making sure that all is ready for the first meal preparation of the first pre-dawn visit to the kitchen. It's a strange irony that the month of fasting from food and drink creates so much obsession with food and drink. My experience of Ramadan has been in a hot, dry climate and this is what much of the Muslim world experiences. The huge diaspora of Muslims throughout the world, however, now means that they find themselves in all kinds of different climates with longer or shorter daylight hours, with different kinds of foods and culinary longings. But the habits are there and the prophet's example established, so wherever you are, there are sure to be tasty dates at hand, the prophet's chosen preference for breaking the fast at sunset. But there will be other local delicacies that sell well at this time of year. In Meskine there are various forms of fried cakes and pastries, fresh fruits and salads, meat, fish and chicken in abundance, lots of sugar to sweeten the tea and the millet drink, and blocks of ice to cool down the water for the first thirst-quenching guzzle as the call to prayer rings out at sunset.

What essentially happens during Ramadan is an exchange of daytime for night-time and night-time for daytime, as far as eating goes. At 3 a.m. there will be the call from the mosque to get people off their beds, the call to the women to get into the kitchen to prepare the pre-sunrise meal. What this meal contains will vary from household to household. It could simply be a millet-based hot drink like a thin porridge, or it could be a full-blown meal with meat or fish sauce and millet. Once this meal has been forced down into the stomach that has not yet woken up, it will be time to pray the sunrise prayer ritual. No more eating or drinking now until sunset. In a hot, dry climate this is an awfully long time; pity the ones who live in 40 degrees C or more, which is the case in Meskine when

Ramadan coincides with the hottest months of the year. But the local understanding of 'the tougher it is, the more reward from Allah you will receive' keeps the community focused on getting through the month with remarkably few complaints.

From this time on, the day is a series of ritual prayers, attending the mosque to hear the Qur'an being read and translated into the local language, listening to the imam preach at the mosque or on the radio, and sleeping. If there is someone you need to visit or an errand that needs to be done, then it will preferably be done in the morning. Those who have a job or work at the markets will carry on pretty much as normal, but will take a longer time to do the ritual prayers, as the repetitions are increased during Ramadan. I have noticed that the roads are generally much quieter from midday onwards, as the sun gets hotter and the two afternoon prayer times approach. This is the time when there really is nothing else you can do but sleep; your thirst is telling you to drink, your body is getting weary from the lack of night-time sleep and your belly is beginning to tell you to eat something. This is the time of day when you have to tell yourself that the great reward you are striving for will be worth it in the end. The market traders are snoozing at their posts, the wives and mothers are taking a nap at home with the children, heads are spinning, tongues are parched and conversation is hard work.

Once the afternoon prayer ritual is done by about 4 p.m. it's as though a switch has been turned on and people have a new burst of energy; thirst, hunger and tiredness are distracted by the preparation of food that is required for the evening. The chatter at home begins again, the markets burst into life and there is a collective sense of relief as sunset draws near. The women get busy preparing food from mid-afternoon onwards, especially those who produce fried delicacies to sell in the pre-sunset, frenzied market.

Then it finally comes, the call from the mosque to tell you that it is officially over until tomorrow morning. As the prayer call is being made there will be that first wonderful long drink, the children who are learning how to fast being the first to partake. The more experienced will finish their prayer ritual first and not make a big scene about having a drink. The eating and drinking that follows, though, is celebratory – shared with generosity and a sense of reward for the hard work of the day. There will be several waves of eating throughout the evening, the first being the drink, then the dates and fried cakes, then the fruits and salads, and then the big meal with meat sauce and millet, maize or rice, all finished off with sweet tea. There will be another prayer ritual sandwiched between these various waves of eating and drinking, and then it is all done until early the next morning. This is a cycle that is repeated for twenty-eight, twenty-nine or thirty days, depending on when the imams decide they have seen the narrow crescent of the new moon in the night sky, signalling the end of Ramadan.

So what drives people to such lengths, such control over their physical appetites, such careful attention to being good and without sin for a month every year? As with everything in Islam, it is a striving to obey the rules that they believe have been set down by the prophet Mohammad in the Qur'an and collected writings of the Hadith. The month of Ramadan is thought to be the month when a Muslim can gain so much more credit and reward from God for their good deeds and adherence to religious law and practice than at any other time of the year. Consequently, there is a firm belief that if you are at your holiest during this time of year it will make up for all the other eleven months when you are not so holy. It's all about reward and getting those divine weighing scales moving in your favour – for the 'good deeds' side to be heavier than the 'bad deeds' side. The salvation of your soul depends on your efforts to be good, holy, obedient and submitted to Allah. It's all about what you can do to please God so you can escape the eternal flames of hell. So if you think your eternal destination depends on your own efforts then, of course, you will be driven with all your heart and soul to be the holiest you possibly can be in this blessed month of Ramadan.

I have talked to many people in Meskine about their motivation during Ramadan and have received many different responses. One of my neighbours summed it up when she explained to me what kept her going during the fasting month: 'How benevolent of Allah to give humankind this opportunity to win extra reward to pay the debt of all the previous eleven months of sin and shame.' For her that was all the motivation she needed, year after year.

I have asked my Fulbe friends many times if they really believe that what they are doing in Ramadan will make God love them more and allow them into heaven. Some answer with confidence that God himself asks us to do this, so he must love us more if we do it. It is commanded, we are doing it for God and therefore there will be a reward. Others answer with uncertainty, saying no one can know for sure that they will get to heaven, only God knows that; but they will do what is required by Islam because it can't be bad, can it? Some will say confidently that this month of Ramadan is so profitable and blessed that every prayer ritual completed, every verse of the Qur'an recited, every good deed done, every help given to the poor during this month is worth multiple times more (the quantity will vary depending on who you ask) during this month than in any of the other eleven months of the year. If you die in this month, you are blessed. If you are born in this month, you are blessed. Many of my Muslim friends believe that the prayer ritual completed on the last day of Ramadan is worth so much more reward than the very same prayer ritual they will do the next day not in Ramadan. Such is the wonder that this month holds to the Fulbe and other Muslims around the world.

Having spent numerous Ramadans among the Fulbe, I never fail to be impressed by the depth of commitment that is shared by the community to adhere to their religious traditions. Alongside this, though, I can't miss noticing the irony that what is verbally said to be an exercise in humility actually has the opposite effect for many. All this dependence on one's own effort and strength, strivings and works can become very self-obsessive, so it is not at all surprising to feel the cloud of pride that hangs over a Muslim community at this time. The enemy of our souls knows how to lure humans into this trap of thinking of oneself more highly than one should. A month that is theoretically meant to be a month of humbling oneself into submission to Allah and all that is 'good' turns into a festival of nightly indulgence and a celebration of daily self-control, self-congratulation and sense of great relief over all that has been achieved by sheer willpower.

With a whole community following the same rhythm during Ramadan there is an incredibly strong sense of belonging to something much bigger than yourself. It's as though there is an almost tangible force, a wave, pushing and pulling Muslims along to conformity. The expectation is immovable; a true and good Muslim will conform and fulfil the expectations of the month of Ramadan, if physically able. If you are not physically able you will be missing out, but don't worry as you can pay back your debt when you are feeling better. It is so important to take part in Ramadan that it becomes a part of your identity.

My outsider's eyes, though, have observed some rather disturbing things that seem to be the very opposite of what is being strived for during Ramadan, that longed-for holiness in thought and deed. One year a boy was murdered in a local mosque. He was a *talibi*, a student at a qur'anic school, sent there as a young boy of about 7 years old, a long way from his family and village. These boys study the Qur'an at the end of a whip and are sent to beg on the streets for money and food. One Ramadan, this boy was with a group of his fellow *talibi*s and a fight broke out among them. They were in the mosque at prayer time during the day, so there were many grown men there too, but the fight among the children was not stopped and one of these boys died right there in the mosque during Ramadan. What a horrific tragedy!

It is also known that terrorist groups in recent years have increased their killing sprees during Ramadan,[1] thinking they are pleasing Allah by killing people in his name during this holiest month. Their motivation is fuelled by the notion that they are honouring God by killing people who oppose their form of Islam, and there is no better time to do so than during the holiest month in their calendar.

It is my observation that poorer people are the most wretched and the most tired during Ramadan. They are already used to only having two meals at most each day anyway, so this is no different, but the fact that you can't drink either and still have to work is the hardest of all. The fields still need to be ploughed, the markets frequented to sell your meagre goods, the animals still pastured, and all this still done under the harsh sun. If you are wealthy, then you can shelter away from it, but not if you are poor. It is not unknown for the elderly poor to become so weak from fasting that they die during Ramadan, seen as a blessing, of course, by many. But it begs us to ask the question: Does God really want us to precipitate our own deaths by lack of water?

And what about the Ramadan marriages? Just before Ramadan I have observed a great rush and burst of weddings as men seek to have a wife in time for Ramadan, or a new virgin wife to have alongside his older wives. Why the rush? Well, a man needs a cook to prepare the food early in the morning during Ramadan, so if he doesn't have a wife yet, or has just divorced a previous wife, then he needs one for the month that is coming. Another factor is that visiting prostitutes is forbidden during Ramadan, so men want to make sure they have a woman at home to meet their sexual needs; a wife is therefore required. Physical pleasure at night is, after all, not frowned upon during this month, so if a man can have a lovely new young wife, then what better way to ease the discomfort of the day. Sadly, the reality is that these marriages often don't last, and there is almost as much rejection of these new brides after Ramadan as there is welcoming them before. Divorce in the following months is almost to be expected.

With the cumulative effect of observing so many Ramadans in Cameroon, I have an unsettled feeling when I know it is on its way again. My heart becomes heavy and sad. There is this collective rejection of God's grace, which is the gift of salvation, and not by works, so that no one should boast.[2] Instead, there is a swell of pride that rises from the community that I find heartbreaking at times. Constant calls come from the mosques day and night to carry out the prayer rituals, to follow the 'straight path', to submit to Allah – and yet I don't see the change of heart that leads to true freedom for souls. These words of Paul come to mind when I see the effects of Ramadan: 'Such regulations indeed have an appearance of wisdom, with their self-imposed worship, their false humility and their harsh treatment of the body, but they lack any value in restraining sensual indulgence' (Col. 2:23).

I do not see a transformation of the Muslim world when a couple of billion people have collectively tried to be holy and good. The poor remain poor, much of the Muslim world remains at the brink of war and in turmoil, the rich are as indulgent as ever, children are still dying because of unclean water, divorce and abuse are rampant, murder in the name of God who has commanded us not to murder is seen as 'holy'. It is true that an outsider's view of so-called Christian culture may come up with many conclusions that are hard to digest, too, and I am not proposing that non-Muslim cultures are without guilt when it comes to issues of justice and taking care of the poor. I do, however, want to put the thought out there that if Ramadan is meant to be an exercise in moving towards purity, then how many more centuries will it take for the Islamic community to heal itself? I suggest that it cannot, just as the rest of the world cannot heal or save itself either.

Conquering a person's sinful desires can only be done by the power of God at work in our lives, and this can only come through faith in the One he has sent who conquered the power of sin and death. This is Jesus Christ. The holiness that Muslims strive for cannot be attained through human power and strength. We must look to God who clothes us with his righteousness and his holiness, through Jesus Christ; not our righteousness, as ours is way below the standard required and infinitely flawed. Our efforts at righteousness and holiness do not change our hearts, but just deceive us into thinking we have been righteous and holy. Sadly, the reality is so different.

The desperation of the hope of eternal life without assurance that manifests itself during the month of Ramadan was never more tangible throughout the rest of the year than during an event that became very much a part of our daily lives in Meskine.

14

Death and Funerals

Before I came to Cameroon I had not been face to face with death very much and I think I was fairly typical of other young adults from my culture. True enough, coming from a medical training and background, I was occasionally alongside death in the workplace. I had seen dead bodies, and I had even been present when patients had passed from life to death, taking their final breath. But somehow I was able to detach myself from the enormity of it. In my family there had been some deaths, with my great-grandparents, grandparents, friends of my parents, and even a friend of mine, which were all more painful than the deaths of my patients at work. A death that touched me deeply was that of a little boy who lived next door to us when I was about 14 years old. The finality of death hit me for the first time; the earthly life that had been so vibrant was now over, nothing could be added to it and nothing taken away.

In contrast, life in Cameroon seems to be constantly in touch with death. Visiting the dying, attending funerals and greeting those bereaved is a very important and major part of social interaction. The more I experience this, the more I objectively see my own culture and realize that death holds a much quieter, more private place in my English home than in Cameroon.

Physically being with those close to the dead or dying is simply irreplaceable in Cameroon; it is the most welcomed and honouring thing you can do. It doesn't matter how long after the event you hear about a loved one passing, even years after the death your visit to greet the bereaved is priceless. It is a show of respect for the one who died, an acknowledgement that their life was important, that you understand their parting was painful for the family. But most of all to the Fulbe, it shows that you want the one who has passed to be allowed into heaven, so you go to add your plea and prayer to the hundreds of others by asking God to forgive them and grant them passage to paradise. Because assurance of salvation is absent in Islam this side of the grave, these pleas on behalf of the dead are seen to be of great value, even necessary, to tip the balance of God's judgement in favour of the dead. There is a phrase that echoes through the crowds over and over again at funerals as they come to greet the family of the dead: 'May God forgive them and grant them heaven,' followed by the 'Amen' of all those around.

When it seems that there is still hope that someone who is ill may recover, family members come together to pool their resources to get the patient to medical care. Tragically, though, there is the scenario, often repeated, of too little, too late: as the last dying gasps are being made, the family wants to be seen to be doing something, so they rush to the hospital. More times than I care to count I can recall a great flurry of activity as a family carries in their sick relative to the hospital only to discover they had already died on the way, or literally took their last breath as they walked over the hospital threshold. The story would often be told of a long history of illness over weeks, if not months: 'Doctor, we tried everything; we bought medicines at the market, we tried our Fulbe medicine, we took them to the local healer, but they didn't get better, so we have now brought them to you. But you see, it was God's will that they died. There's nothing you can do if it is God's will.' And the thought that comes shooting into my mind is, 'If only they had brought them earlier.' Another family leaves to bury their dead, believing that they had done everything they could.

When illness has come upon someone and the family has brought them to the hospital, there is at least hope. However, some do not get better but rather weaker and weaker, and as all hope seems to fade and death seems inevitable, there is a practical air of resignation that comes over the family. It is not surprising that most families at our hospital, when they realize their loved one is dying, prefer to take them home as soon as possible so they can die at home. Without wanting to sound flippant, this has practical connotations as much as anything, as it is easier to transport someone who is still alive than to transport a corpse. Things need to be done in preparation: the sheet to wrap the body in and the grass mat to wrap up the enshrouded body need to be bought. The imam needs to be called to pray, the relatives need to be there to part with their loved one, as maybe there are last words that need to be heard. The family also want to know that they died as a good Muslim saying the *Shahada*, the confession of the Muslim faith. Ultimately, the dying person needs to be facing towards Mecca as they take their final breath. The body needs to be washed. A vehicle must be found to take the body to be buried. A few strong men need to dig the grave. Fulbe like to bury their dead as soon as possible after death – the same day if it is daylight, or at first light if the death occurred during the night. Once someone has died, there is a lot to be done and there are no undertakers or funeral services to help with these tasks.

When the body is buried there are three days of mourning when everyone comes to greet the family, gathered in their respective groups: spouses and children, parents and siblings, uncles, aunties and cousins, and the in-laws. Women relatives will be sitting inside the compound in the houses; the men will be sitting on mats in the shade outside the entrance to the compound.

These first three days are when most emotion is displayed. A woman arriving on hearing of the death will be quiet and controlled, but as soon as she enters the house where her close relatives are, she will suddenly burst into loud wailing and crying. Only after a few minutes, with other women around telling her to be patient and stop crying because it is God's will that the loved one died, will she then control herself again and quietly greet each woman in the room. The ritual greetings go around and around as each woman enters, 'There has been a terrible disaster, we have suffered a great loss; our father has left us but he has only followed the road that we must all follow. He has gone before us. We must be patient. There is nothing we can do. It is God's will. May God forgive him and grant him heaven.' These phrases are repeated over and over again, like a well-rehearsed formula they come spilling out. As a visitor and foreigner to this culture, some of the hardest things for me to learn were which phrases to say when, to whom and how to behave at a funeral.

There is something intense about these gatherings and, for one stumbling over the Fulfulde words, seeing this sea of women packed into a crowded, sweltering room feels very intimidating. First, trying to find the woman who is the chief mourner in the room is a task in itself; all the women are covered up, hiding behind their veils, and it often seems so dark as you step into these rooms from the bright sunshine outside until your eyes have adjusted to the shade. I was always very grateful to see a friendly, familiar face outside the room who offered to take me in and introduce me to the women I should be greeting! I had to try not to show my great joy at seeing my friend though, as it's not appropriate to smile until you have finished greeting. Then you can talk about anything you like, much to my astonishment on many occasions.

I decided early on that I could not bring myself to say all of the expected script. Sometimes I just could not agree that it was necessary that the person died. I could not say 'it had to be' because I knew medically that there had been a solution, if only it had been sought earlier, if at all. The hardest of these times were the funerals of babies and little children who had faded away with malnutrition, dehydration or anaemia often secondary to malaria. It's true that these little ones can become so ill so quickly, the family taken by surprise and not ready to go to the hospital. Not having cash in hand has led to many of these little ones dying. Dad says he will sell the goat in the morning in order to have cash to go to the hospital, only to be left with his dead child in his arms during the night. So, as I would sit at the funeral hearing the echo going around, 'It had to be, there was nothing that could be done,' I would feel a mixture of sadness and anger, knowing full well that it did not have to be and there was plenty that could have been done. But this was not the place or the time to say so. Only afterwards, a few weeks later, would I broach the subject and ask the mother what had happened. Her face would tell the story, sadness in her eyes reflecting her broken heart; she knew only too well that there was so much more that could have been done, if only they had been prepared, if only her husband had agreed to take the child to hospital earlier.

One dear friend of mine, a devout Muslim, lost her little girl in exactly this situation. Talking to her, I could see that this pain of loss would be with her forever, but her words struck me deeper still as I asked her why she had not been able to take her little girl to the hospital. 'This was my husband's child and I had no power to make that decision. He had no money that day so what could I do? I have to accept that this was God's will for my baby; if not then I am arguing with God and who am I to do that? This was God's will for me and my baby.' She said this to me through her tears, trying to convince herself that this was the only answer that she could live with for the rest of her life. Her mother walked in as we were talking and reprimanded her daughter for still crying over the dead child so many days after the death. It's permissible to cry during the first three days but not after that, as it is showing you have not accepted God's will. I left my friend's home that day with the realization that using 'God's will' when responsibility has been neglected was the local culture's answer to a guilty conscience when guilt cannot be acknowledged. To acknowledge guilt is too shameful, and too painful to carry around for the rest of your life.

The other phrase that I struggle to say at funerals is the echo, 'May God forgive him and grant him heaven.' The pursuit of the safe place where your soul can rest for eternity is the reason for most religious journeys. That longing deep down to know that all will be well beyond the grave, that what you fear most, whether it be nothingness or eternal burning, will be replaced by peace and a final end to pain and suffering. For others, it is the longing to finally be in the unbroken presence of God and sharing in all his goodness and abundance, where sin and death can no longer destroy. Fulbe are no different in their search and it is finally at the funeral where an earthly journey has come to an end that the uncertainty is left hanging in the air. Did my loved one do enough on this earth to get passage into heaven? What if his good deeds were not enough? There is an obligation for the living to keep pleading and praying for the dead, to help them out with any deficit, so that on that Judgement Day the weighing scales will fall in their favour and passage will be granted.

Once I was having a heart-to-heart talk with a long-time Fulbe friend who had experienced the power of God's love through Jesus in her life several times. She believed what Jesus had done for her on the cross and the power of his resurrection, and remained forever grateful. She was not, however, intentional in growing in her faith and remained isolated from other Fulbe believers in Jesus for the rest of her life. On this day she had come to stay with me for a few days, so we had more uninterrupted time to talk than we were used to, which led to deeper conversation. I asked my friend why she still felt the need to *juulugo* (the ritual five-times-a-day prayers of Islam) if she really believed Jesus had already done the work of salvation for her. It was something I had been wanting to ask her for a long time, but there never seemed to be the right moment without it sounding like harsh criticism. Her answer that day shone a light on Fulbe uncertainty about death and the obligation of the living.

She recounted to me how her dying mother had made her promise to pray for the souls of her mother and her father every time she did her Muslim prayers. 'Please remember us, my child, for the rest of your days; every time you pray the *salat*, pray for our souls that we will be forgiven and granted heaven on that final day.' As any dutiful daughter would, she promised as she watched her mother fading away. She therefore felt this obligation to keep praying the Muslim prayers, even though she no longer believed it had any benefit for her own salvation; by doing so she still hoped that somehow it would benefit her parents' souls. This hope of heaven after death, without assurance, casts a shadow over the living. That is why it is an oft-repeated refrain at the funerals, 'Merciful God, forgive him and grant him heaven.'

The overwhelming desire to know where your final destination will be comes to the fore when illness strikes and your mortality is starkly obvious. Those of us working in the medical profession are alongside people day after day as they work through the inevitable conclusion that modern medicine can't cure all ills. It has been frustrating to many visiting doctors to Meskine that illnesses that would be treatable to a certain extent in their home cultures, such as some forms of cancer, are just not treatable here due to lack of accessible medicines. One such case was a middle-aged lady named Fadi. Dr Jacqueline had done all she could to treat this lady who had developed leukaemia, but the prognosis was not good.

Fadi was a pleasant, chatty neighbour of ours and often visited our home in the evenings for a short while before she got too sick to leave her home. It became clear that Fadi was dying and she herself realized this. During one evening visit she was unusually open about her sadness, expressing that she was not ready to die yet. More than anything, she declared that she was afraid to die because she didn't know if she had done enough to please God in her lifetime. I took the opportunity to share with her the hope that I have found in Jesus, knowing that he had already paid for my sin and opened the way for us to go to heaven. Jacqueline had previously tried to share this good news with Fadi but had not found her willing to listen with an open heart. This time too, I found that she was just unable to receive it, but was still clinging to the system of belief that gave no assurance.

However, as I was explaining my hope after death to Fadi, it was as if God was wanting to speak to my own heart. As I spoke, I felt as if I was sitting next to Fadi and listening to myself, and then in my mind I was questioning what I was saying: 'Do you really believe this? Do you really know without a doubt where you are going when you die?' My own thoughts shocked me! Here I was in Meskine for the sole purpose of pointing people to Jesus who is our hope and salvation, and yet I had not really worked through my own doubts and feelings about my own death and mortality. That evening I asked God to give me that absolute assurance and confidence in the gospel, to know that Jesus is all I need. I did not imagine that a couple of weeks later I would be back in the UK and find myself attached to a ventilator in intensive care, fighting for my life! God used this sudden acute neurological incident to teach me that, indeed, Jesus is more than enough in the face of death. The extraordinary peace that I experienced during the days, months and years that followed is a treasure that has enriched my life beyond measure. I know without a shadow of doubt that Jesus is who he said he is. He is the resurrection and the life; he is the only one who can assure us of life after death and peace for the journey (John 11:25–6).

In the light of this personal experience, it therefore moves me deeply to hear so many pleas at funerals for the forgiveness of the one who has died. When I contrast it with the funerals of followers of Jesus I have been to in Cameroon, and in my own home culture, the difference could not be greater. There is such a confidence in our hope after death, such assurance that Jesus has already done enough, such a reality that God's gift of grace poured out upon us is sufficient to render the weighing scales of our deeds redundant. We no longer need to fear death but can welcome it as our final homecoming to our heavenly Father. That echo of 'God forgive him and grant him heaven' will not be heard at these funerals because it is not necessary. How we respond to God's gift of grace in Christ while we are living on earth is what counts, not the pleas of the ones we leave behind when we die. It's too late by then.

One of the most powerful parables of Jesus addresses this issue, that of the rich man and poor Lazarus in Luke 16:19–31. Both have died and been judged: the rich man finds himself in Hades, the place of torment, while Lazarus finds himself in the presence of Abraham, a place of comfort. Abraham explains to the rich man that there is no way for his circumstances to be changed now, as a great chasm separates the tormented from the comforted. As the rich man realizes his terrible mistake in rejecting the way of salvation while he was on earth, he asks for Lazarus to be allowed to return to earth to warn the rest of the rich man's family, so that they might escape the same fate. But Jesus says it clearly in this arresting parable: the living have all they need to find the way out of torment before they die. They have the words of Moses and the prophets, who God has given to show the way. If people choose to ignore them and turn away while they are on earth then they have missed the opportunity God has given. Even sending them someone who has returned from the grave would not convince them! After death is too late. It's just too late to plead for them then – it's already over.

So, with the echo going on all around me, I have to find other things to say at these funerals. I want to be truthful but I don't want to offend; I want to be loving and represent Jesus. After all, I don't actually know where the dead person stood in God's eyes; only God knows that. So I try to comfort the living, 'May God comfort your hearts; may you know his loving presence with you; may he give you patience as you come to terms with your loss; may he give you strength.'

I will never forget one special funeral. It was the third day of mourning for a friend in Meskine. She had become a follower of Jesus about a year before, albeit a rather 'secret believer', and had been baptized quietly with a few other Fulbe believers one evening. Her life had been full of sorrow and pain, some caused by things done to her and some caused by her own decisions. She had become lost and alone. Divorced three times, rather estranged from her only daughter, extremely poor and recently found to be HIV-positive, she had finally died in pain from cancer. But she had met Jesus in a wonderful way from reading about him in the Bible during the last months of her life – it changed her forever. She understood the finality of Jesus' work on the cross and his power over sin, death and evil. The person of Jesus became a reality to her and gave her genuine peace and joy at the end of her earthly life.

'How do you know what you are reading is true?' Jacqueline and I asked her one day.

She replied with a glowing smile on her tired face, 'I just know. I believe all that you have told me about Jesus and all that I have read. It's all in my heart.'

At her funeral, there we all were, sitting for the final prayer from the imam on the third day. The crowd of men from the neighbourhood and her male relatives sitting on the mats under the trees at the entrance to the compound; and crowds of women sitting on mats in the rooms and outside the buildings in the sun. The imam was mumbling the Arabic prayer with the men, out of earshot of the women, but we all raised our hands, palms up to show we were joining in. But that day, three of us in the crowd were praying something else in our hearts: two other Fulbe followers of Jesus who had known our friend and read the Bible and prayed with her, and me. We sat together in the crowd and, as we lifted our hands, we were thanking God in our hearts for the life of our dear sister who was now safely home with her heavenly Father and with Jesus.

We just knew. We believed it. We left the funeral that day missing our sister but rejoicing that we didn't need to join in the echo of pleading God's forgiveness for her. It was already done and we just knew we would be seeing her again one day.

Another remarkable funeral that showed the difference that knowing Jesus makes was that of a 5-year-old little girl, Esther. It had been a happy day at church when suddenly a hidden disaster struck. The church community was celebrating Christmas and New Year with a concert from the women's group one Sunday afternoon. The church was packed and the whole place was full of life as we clapped and danced while the women sang. The dust rose from the earth floor, the drum beat and hearty voices burst out of the room with joy. But throughout that day it became apparent that the pastor's dog was not well and was becoming increasingly bad-tempered. It had bitten several people already and that afternoon, while all the singing and dancing was going on, Esther was also bitten by the dog on her face. The pastor himself was later bitten on his hand while trying to get the dog under control. As the day went on it became clear that the dog was dying with rabies. For sure it had been vaccinated; the pastor, having been a veterinary nurse before his pastoral training, had been very vigilant at keeping his animals' vaccinations up to date. It was therefore with a deepening horror that day that he finally had to get the dog killed.

Those who had been bitten were taken to Meskine Hospital, a few yards down the road, to get their wounds cleaned and the injections to fight rabies. Then the long wait began. Once you are bitten by a rabid animal, it can take days or weeks for symptoms of infection to show. Many prayers were said during those anxious weeks, for healing and protection.

Sadly, after a couple of weeks, little Esther started to develop the symptoms of rabies: aversion to light, difficulty swallowing as her muscles tightened up, and fever. This little girl finally succumbed to the disease after two days and died in her mother's arms at the hospital. A great sadness touched everyone on the staff at the hospital, as Esther's father was one of their colleagues; the church community and the wider village were also deeply saddened. Then there was the inner panic of the others who had been bitten too; would they also develop the deadly illness? As the days turned to weeks, it became clear that it was only little Esther, in the end, who would.

Her funeral was a very moving experience. As her small coffin was resting on a table in front of her house, the whole area around her family's home was packed with people who had come to share the family's grief. Relatives, friends from church, colleagues from the hospital, neighbours and just people from the village who felt the deep sadness of the occasion, many of whom were Muslims, all gathered together. The director of the funeral service was the same pastor and neighbour whose dog had bitten Esther. One could only imagine the sadness in his heart that day, and yet here he was encouraging everyone with the hope that knowing Jesus brings beyond the grave. As we sang the popular song in Fulfulde, 'Heaven is our home; there is no suffering there', I could not stop the tears from welling up in my eyes and I was not the only one. Yet there was this beautiful sense of peace and hope, a priceless, quiet joy that pervaded the whole gathering. What a contrast it was to the many funerals I had attended in the same village, often with some of the same people, when there was no assurance of being with God, no peace. I know which road I would rather be on, and I believe many Muslims went home that day after Esther's funeral with many thoughts of their own spiritual journey. For many of them it was the first time they had been present at a funeral of a non-Muslim and the stark contrast to what they had been used to could not have been clearer.

There are few events in Meskine that demonstrate the strength of the community quite like a funeral. Nobody lives in isolation in this village. In one way or another you are part of the community, be it because of your family connections, your occupation, your religion or your tribe. When MCWA moved into this place it was therefore not surprising that it would impact this community in one way or another. What has unfolded in the relationship between Meskine Hospital and the community over the years though, has turned out to be rather surprising.

15

How to Change a Village

One late afternoon in 2017, I was enjoying wandering around the wards, chatting and greeting patients and their families. It was a rare opportunity, as we were not in Meskine very often since the MCWA team had had to leave three years earlier due to the insecurity. As I reached the private rooms at the back of the ward, I was greeted by a man I recognized as a previous neighbour of mine in the village. He had been born in Meskine and lived here all his life; consequently, he had watched the hospital arrive and develop over the years.

My neighbour was at the hospital taking care of his brother who had undergone some surgery and was now recovering. He called me in to sit with him and his brother, 'Madam Kerry, there's something I want to tell you. Please sit down.'

So I perched on the stool next to his brother's bed and, after we had greeted, waited to hear what was coming next . . . Was he going to ask for money to pay the hospital bill? Was he going to tell me that we needed to move back to Meskine? Was he simply being friendly as we hadn't seen each other for a long time? What came next rather caught me by surprise.

'For many years the people in Meskine have not appreciated this hospital. We have often overlooked it and gone to other health centres further away as we thought we knew better. We thought that we didn't need your hospital. But now that all you foreigners have left and we see that our Cameroonian brothers and sisters are still doing such a great job, we have learned to appreciate this place. They still love us and care for us, and the patients get better and come home well. Finally, after all these years, we people in Meskine appreciate this place. We used to call it "white people's hospital" but, Kerry, I'm telling you that is not true. It is now "our hospital". This place belongs to the people of Meskine and we will protect it and defend it. I'm telling you, I will protect this hospital with my life if I have to!'

This short conversation illustrates the progress that has been made over twenty-five years in the relationship between Meskine village and the hospital. In many ways Meskine is an insignificant village, not quite out in the isolated bush and not quite in the bustling town. It doesn't have anything remarkable about it other than having its very own *lamiido* (king or chief), and having a beautiful northern view of the surrounding hills. The electricity supply can be challenging at times, especially in the rainy season, and the wells tend to dry up in the dry season. It's not a place where the rich and famous would choose to live, but to many it is home and the place where they belong. The name 'Meskine' itself is not at all glorious; it comes from the Arabic word *miskin*, meaning 'poor, wretched, humble', so that must tell us something of its history. In the great plan of our great God, it was to this place that he led MCWA to build a hospital. Inevitably, having a thriving medical institution in the village has impacted the identity and course of the community over the years, so much so that now, when the village of Meskine is mentioned in a conversation, the subject often veers towards the hospital that Meskine hosts. It would be difficult to imagine the village without the hospital now, or the hospital without the village, as the two communities have become entwined together.

Employment and Economy

One of the unspoken expectations of the villagers when MCWA first arrived was that the unfolding medical project would provide many jobs for the locals; this was a welcome dream held by many. The majority of village residents were farmers or traders and still are today; many children did not get beyond a few years of primary school, if that. Unemployment was the norm, and it was up to each individual to invent a way of life and create something new. The thought, therefore, of getting a job with an actual monthly salary was very appealing. Even today, twenty-five years later, this is still the greatest hope and desire for most Cameroonians: 'If I could only get a job with a salary, then I know life would become better.' Happily, some of the people from the village were able to find employment at the hospital, but not as many as expected.

The reality was that many of the village residents were not qualified for such work, with very low schooling levels. At the beginning of the construction work some local people found employment as labourers, but when the call went out for applicants for nursing training it was a different story. In order to be fair, the team set the standard for applicants as having achieved five levels of senior school, regardless of their religion, tribe or village. This inadvertently meant that the majority of medical employees ended up coming from places outside of Meskine. Most of the first nurses came from the hill tribes nearby. Even among the builders, guards and cleaners it was rare to find a local, original Meskine resident. So many workers coming in from other places led to an influx of new residents in the village, and with each employee came their family. Each family would need a home – and so began the house building boom on the northern side of the village where the hospital was situated.

Whole new neighbourhoods were developed as one by one the hospital employees built their houses. They came to Meskine as mostly young and unmarried, full of enthusiasm for life as they travelled around on their bicycles; as the years rolled by they got married, had children, and traded their bikes in for motorcycles and cars. The houses grew as quickly as the children did. As most of these new families were Christians, they also brought their church denomination with them. Before the hospital was built there was one Protestant and one Catholic church on the outskirts of the village; it was not long before others sprung up and five more Protestant churches were soon full. It's not surprising that, with all this growth and change, there was some resentment from the local population, and challenges arose as these new people learned to live alongside the original residents of the village. Generally, however, the community has worked hard to ensure that harmony continues. New friendships have formed and mutual respect has been gained as these Muslims and Christians have learned to live side by side peacefully. The benefit of having a neighbour who works at the hospital has certainly been appreciated by most when a loved one has become unwell. Having a chaperone at your side to guide you through the hospitalization process is always welcome.

With all these new salaried households springing up in the village, the local economy has changed and adapted too. What was once a rather average-sized weekly market-day on Wednesdays has grown to overflowing in the centre of the village. It's a common pattern in these rural places that each larger village or town in the area will have a specific 'market-day' when residents from the more remote villages can bring their wares to sell, and then stock up for their needs at home. For many it's the life-sustaining day, as they make the most profit on these days, and can then in turn feed their families. The upturn in the economy is therefore a benefit for all. As the hospital has grown over the years, the number of patients pouring into the village for medical care has also grown, which in turn has contributed to the local economy. At one point there were so many people coming for medical treatment from Chad that a Meskine businessman built, in front of the hospital, a whole row of new shops and rooms to rent out to Chadian families as temporary accommodation.

Another very visible reminder of the economic effect of the hospital is the daily market that is positioned at its entrance. Right across the street from the main gate is the roofed area where traders are seated selling their wares: fried cakes, kola nuts, onions, tomatoes, vegetables, meat, phone credit, tea, soap, firewood, even cooking pots and sleeping mats. There are a couple of restaurants, too, where you can relax on a mat with a home-from-home meal. In front of all this is the row of waiting motorcycle-taxi men, ready for their next customer; they know this is a sure place to find work.

Village Development

MCWA has always wanted Meskine Hospital to be an advantage for the whole village, and not just tolerated as a private enterprise. Because of this it has looked for ways to build a meaningful relationship with the village and take part in efforts to improve life for residents. This has led to joining in with local road projects and repairs, and local initiatives with health education and vaccination programmes. In 2007, the hospital administrator had a different idea. He suggested that MCWA ask the village chief to recommend a major project that the hospital could undertake on its own, rather than giving several small contributions to different village needs. The chief thought this was an excellent idea and, after discussing with Meskine's development committee, it was suggested that MCWA could build a new classroom for the growing middle school. It was actually going to become a high school, so the timing of this was perfect.

As was the case with many rural schools in the region, the classrooms were often overcrowded, with more than one hundred students per room and five students squashed onto a bench made for three. The village had started to raise money to build this extra classroom but had only got as far as building the walls, and grass mats were being used as a temporary roof. MCWA was more than happy to help and agreed to build another complete classroom. The building team from the hospital constructed it to a high standard and also gave a gift of twenty benches to make it ready for immediate use. The habit of MCWA, whenever a new building was completed and ready to use, was to gather everyone around to thank God for the work that had been done, to pray for God's protection upon it and for the building to be a blessing to those who would be using it. The village chief and development committee were very happy for MCWA to do the same for this new classroom. On that day there was a real sense of achievement as Meskine and MCWA were able to celebrate working together for the good of the village.

The Community of Gorgorea

There is another community in Meskine that MCWA has particularly been involved with since the first team members arrived. It is the community of people with Hansen's disease, commonly known as leprosy. Decades ago, when leprosy was still rampant and destroying lives, it was seen to be wise to relocate leprosy sufferers to live in communities away from the main villages and towns in order to reduce the infection rate. It was understood that once someone had leprosy then they would be infectious for the rest of their lives. Years later, however, it became clear that this was incorrect and that sufferers were only contagious to those who had had long-term contact with them when they were untreated. The legacy of this misunderstanding was many isolated communities of people with the symptoms of leprosy all over the world, living away from their families and friends, forced together to try to find a way to live. When MCWA arrived in Meskine, the team found the little village of Gorgorea and a nearby neighbourhood that was home to around forty people who had been diagnosed with leprosy years before, and had subsequently received medical treatment.

Since the 1970s there has been very effective multi-drug treatment for the disease, which now means that people are saved from life-changing deformities if they are treated early in the disease process. When you see someone for the first time who has had leprosy and suffered the ill effects, it can move you beyond words. Often there is facial disfigurement due to the destruction of the cartilage that gives shape to the nose. They may have visual problems and be constantly wiping their weeping eyes, or have actually become blind. As they shyly offer you their hand in greeting, you may see stumps where useful fingers used to be. This is because of the permanent damage to the nerves of the hands and feet which destroys the protective sense of feeling. You can imagine the destruction that happens to fingers that are tilling the soil or cooking over fire but cannot feel pain, or feet that walk miles with only thin sandals or flip-flops for protection against stones and thorns. By the time such a person has reached middle age there are often no fingers or toes left, which renders them dependent on others for many daily tasks, even eating. It is not unusual for leprosy sufferers to have chronic ulcers on their hands and feet because of this loss of protective pain. They constantly destroy and reinjure a part of their flesh simply because they don't know that it should hurt. For some, these ulcers get so bad that they require amputation of their foot because the wound has become a danger to their very life. Leprosy is a horrible, life-wrecking disease. It was the fear of this terror that drove society to create these communities for leprosy sufferers – out of sight and out of mind.

The new presence of a hospital in Meskine led the local government to ask MCWA to take over the responsibility and care for the leprosy patients in Gorgorea. Dr Oubre had previously seen how Mbingo Baptist Hospital had taken care of a similar community, and he welcomed the opportunity to help now. He contacted a Swiss charity (ALES, *Aide aux Lépreux Emmaüs-Suisse*) to see if they would be interested in supporting MCWA's efforts, and ALES were generous in their support, even providing funds to buy a vehicle to make it easier to access them. Since that time MCWA has been providing their medical care, under the direction of the nurse responsible for leprosy and TB management. Inevitably, it was not only medical needs that needed addressing but also issues of poverty and loss of independence. For those who were still able-bodied and keen to work, efforts were made to enable them to make a viable living for themselves. For others, it seemed more appropriate to help their children gain skills in order to take care of their ailing parents. For others still, it was simply a case of love and compassion in providing housing, food and clothing.

The visits to Gorgorea, at Christmas-time particularly, became a fond tradition, as we loaded up the trucks with gifts of food, toiletries and clothes to distribute 2 kilometres away, down the bumpy, dusty, narrow track to the clump of trees and grass-roofed huts. It was an occasion when the whole community gathered, and time was taken to greet each one, and then together we thanked God for the coming of Jesus.

On another occasion a small group of hospital employees and myself visited Gorgorea to distribute sheep to each person we were responsible for, as an encouragement and boost to their private enterprises. The whole community had come out and sat under the trees in expectation, some on mats, some on little wooden stools, some just on the bare ground. Watching them gather and emerge from their homes was in itself a moving experience; the blind each being led by a small child, those on crutches gently picking their way along the stony, thorny paths, the more energetic and youthful bounding over with shouts of 'Welcome, welcome, welcome!'

That day their names were read out one by one, names that we had got to know and care for, announcing '*Baaba*, here is your sheep!' Then a great shout and cry of joy from everyone, and clapping from those who were able. '*Daada*, here is your sheep!' and again they united in a cry of joy. And so it went on until all thirty-something people had received their sheep. The more sheep that were distributed, the more chaotic it became, so that by the end of the distribution there were sheep running in all directions and children running to round up the sheep all over the gathered area, with shouts of joy and bleating drowning each other out.

It was indeed a day to remember, as were most of our visits to Gorgorea. There is something awesome about being with people who have suffered much and yet have learned to live, still smile and show love. They have taught me so much, and I think I speak for many of the MCWA volunteers who have visited Gorgorea over the years. When you are face to face with poverty and suffering to this extent it will stay with you for the rest of your life. It changes you.

Over the years, the number of leprosy sufferers has thankfully reduced as the disease is now considered treatable and is controlled in most corners of the world. There have been no 'additions' to the residents of this community with leprosy since MCWA arrived in Meskine and, happily, government policy has changed from separation to encouraging relocation of these now elderly people back to their home towns and villages. Some have taken up this offer and gone home after many decades away; but for many, Gorgorea is their home now, and they would not consider living anywhere else. With their children and grandchildren now well-established here, there is even a church and a school for them. What was once a place of isolation has become a home.

The Flood

It was rainy season in August 2000, the time of the heaviest rains known as *loddo duumol*, when the coolness brings relief and the farmers are busy working in the fields tending their precious crops, and some days it does nothing but rain. This Saturday Danny, his wife Frances and Dr Jacqueline were heading back to Meskine, having attended a meeting in the nearby town. They were almost home, but the closer they got to Meskine the more water there seemed to be in the surrounding fields. They were rather surprised to be met by a flooded main road that runs through the village, which forced them to take an indirect route back to the hospital. It seemed that there was water everywhere and it wasn't just because of a rainy day. At that moment, Danny and Frances had no idea that they would not be seeing their house until the next day, as it was situated on the other side of the village and so cut off by the flood.

It turned out that this was a devastating deluge, the flood of a lifetime. Being situated alongside a riverbed has its advantages most of the time, particularly if you are a gardener. Even though the river is completely dry most of the year, the water is at least not too deep down and wells can be dug to irrigate the gardens. But come July and August, water suddenly arrives into the sandy riverbeds, as it rolls down from the newly rained-on hills forty miles away. Most of the time it arrives gently and calmly one day or night, cutting off the neighbourhoods on the far side of the river banks. But in 2000 it came with such strength and force that it overflowed the banks and flooded into whole swathes of the village in the lower areas alongside the river banks and the smaller channels flowing from it. This time the rains had flooded a dam in a village upstream from Meskine. After the gates of the dam were opened to relieve the pressure, villages downstream began to flood, overwhelmed by the volume of water flowing into shallow riverbeds. Opening the dam would have been a quick local decision, so no warning was issued to the unsuspecting villagers downstream.

The result was devastation, knocking down and dissolving most of the mud-built walls and houses in its path, filling up the wells with filthy water, drowning animals, uprooting plants and bushes, and destroying gardens. Besides all this, many lost their food supplies for the coming months that had been stored in the destroyed buildings. In a 2-mile area, 11 neighbourhoods were severely damaged; 1,000 buildings collapsed leaving 400 families without a roof over their heads. Fortunately, it had all happened in the daylight, so loss of life was minimal; sadly there were three deaths, but many more injuries as people tried to escape or had walls fall on them.

As the assessment of damage was carried out in the following days, it became clear that two important things needed to be done: disinfecting the wells so that people had clean drinking water to prevent a cholera outbreak, and rebuilding homes so that they could withstand another flood. MCWA decided to launch an appeal to friends in the USA and UK and there was an astonishing immediate response of gifts of nearly US$50,000. Dr Jacqueline got together with teams from the hospital to go from one area of the flood zone to the next with innumerable bottles of chlorine to pour into latrines and wells. Each well's dimensions needed to be calculated so that enough disinfectant was poured in for the volume of water found. This whole process was done three times in every well and every latrine. Government officials came to inspect the aftermath of the disaster in Meskine and met Dr Jacqueline, who was already busy at work, and asked her to take on the responsibility of disease prevention in the village. The district medical officer helped by supplying her with protocols on how to prevent cholera, typhoid fever and dysentery in times of flood. In the end, with 270 wells and 1,400 latrines treated, there was no epidemic of water-borne diseases in Meskine that year. Long humid days in hot sun turned Dr Jacqueline rather sunburnt, but this very practical gesture of care and love touched many hearts in the village. It opened the door for her to continue health education long after the flood, and established relationships of trust for many years to come.

Danny also jumped into action with a mammoth task. Because of the incredible response of help from MCWA supporters outside of Cameroon, he was able to offer house-rebuilding assistance to every family that had lost a home. Before the rebuilding started though, a team was sent to neighbourhoods to inspect damage and talk to homeowners to determine which houses were legitimately destroyed by the flood, and which had collapsed before the flood happened. Danny then got together a very able team of 80 men who set to work, rebuilding the foundations of 336 homes over the following 7 months. The only requests that Danny made of the recipients of the new homes was that they feed each team of four labourers a filling meal at midday, and that they keep their animals away from the freshly made bricks. In this way there was a real sense of working together with the families, which was much appreciated by all.

This time the houses were built with cement-block foundations, rather than mud, up to five rows of bricks from the base. This would ensure that if the river flooded again then these houses would not fall and be destroyed. Today, as you walk near the river, you will still see these houses testifying to those days when MCWA was able to lend a hand to its neighbours. We can look back on those days with gratitude as it was a special opportunity to demonstrate the love of God in very practical ways. The private enterprise of Meskine Hospital felt privileged to be able to help the village that had given it a home.

There was a touching tribute made to Danny, his team and MCWA at a later date at a gathering of leaders and residents in Meskine. One man stood up and announced that this building project was the first time he had witnessed such an outpouring of generosity and care to people, irrespective of tribe or religion.

What a difference twenty-five years can make.

What a difference Jesus can make.

Postscript

In telling the story of the first twenty-five years of Meskine Hospital, it has inevitably led us to consider what the next years of the work will look like. When I started writing this book I did not know what MCWA would decide for the future, but it was evident that something would have to change to ensure that the medical service could continue. After much discussion and prayer with the field team and among the leaders of MCWA, we are overwhelmed by how God has opened the way to ensure that Meskine Hospital will continue into the future. In January 2020, MCWA gave the hospital to Cameroon Baptist Convention (CBC) with the assurance that what God had started through MCWA would continue. CBC already has many decades of experience in running hospitals and health centres in Cameroon and shares MCWA's vision of inviting others to follow Jesus. In many ways, we have a sense of closure and accomplishment with this transfer of ownership as it was at CBC's Mbingo Hospital that Dr Bert Oubre first got the vision to start a hospital in the far north of Cameroon. So it is with thanksgiving and hope for the future that we entrust our beloved Meskine Hospital into the hands of CBC.

Epilogue

The future story of Meskine Hospital is still being written as each day goes by, but the story of the past is an offering of thanksgiving to God for all that he has done. For every patient who has been healed, every life saved or extended, every new baby welcomed into the world, every heart that has received Jesus Christ, every walk with God that has taken on new meaning, every resident of Meskine village who has somehow benefited, I and the rest of the MCWA family thank God and give him all the glory. That he would invite unremarkable people like us from scattered corners of the globe to gather in Meskine to be part of this story only adds to the awe and wonder we have experienced. Our lives testify that following Jesus to the ends of the earth is a privilege, though sometimes wrapped in struggle, and always worth it.

As I draw this book to a close, I am well aware of the detached feeling that can arise after you have read about other people's adventures and exploits in a faraway land, even if some of the people mentioned in the story are known to you. It is very possible to conclude that these are nice stories, that those involved did their best to make a success of things and that on the whole God was somehow honoured in what they were doing. 'But what has that got to do with me?' you might be thinking, as you close this book for the last time. Maybe you are feeling rather grateful that God did not call you to go to Cameroon or to the Fulbe people, and that the MCWA team relieved you of that responsibility by getting there before you. You might be thinking that Meskine, Cameroon and the Fulbe people are simply exotic, distant details on God's earth that you can read about but will never be a part of your life. In conclusion, however, I would like to suggest the opposite, specifically to readers of this book who also call themselves followers of Jesus Christ.

The dramatic and mysterious crescendo of the Bible is the book of Revelation in which the apostle John reveals what God has shown him about the end of time. The image of Jesus being presented with his bride (Rev. 19:7; 21:2,9) is referred to and Paul also alludes to this in his letter to the Ephesians (Eph. 5:22–32). It is a glorious picture of the followers of Jesus being presented to him as his beloved; we, having been made perfect and righteous by the blood of Jesus Christ, have been made ready for him, our bridegroom who is waiting for us. Another image presented in Revelation is the multitudes before the throne of God (Rev. 7:9), people from every tribe and tongue and nation, worshipping him together as one. In my mind's eye it is as if the bride is wearing a multicoloured, beautiful, jewel-adorned robe as she is presented to her bridegroom, and we – the followers of Christ from every different corner of this earth from Baton Rouge to Meskine and everywhere between and beyond – are those beautiful jewels. If one of us were absent then the robe would not be complete and would be less beautiful, and the bride would not be ready to be presented to Jesus.

With this in mind, I encourage you to see yourself as part of the story of this book that you have just read. You may never meet a Pullo on this earth; you may never have the privilege of visiting Cameroon or Meskine, but you will be standing with your Fulbe brothers and sisters in Christ on that incredible day, when we are finally in the unbroken presence of Almighty God. What a day that will be! There is no doubt that the Fulbe jewels on that robe will be shining brightly, just as the jewels of all the other as yet 'unreached people groups' of the earth will be, and the jewels of the ethnic group you align yourself with. The individuals that you have been reading about in this book are just a small glimpse of what God is doing in our world right now to bring about what he has promised to do in building his church. We also are part of this work and all have a part to play.

There will never be a time this side of Jesus' return when the need to share the good news of Jesus is irrelevant. The question for each one of us to ask ourselves is, 'What can I be doing right now to get the bride of Christ ready?' The emerging Fulbe church, the wider church in Cameroon, the church in Louisiana, the church in the UK, the church in China, the church in France, the church that meets in your house or in the pub next door – we all have a job to do because we all belong, as jewels on that robe. All are invited, even commanded, to invite others to meet Jesus. As Jesus sent out his disciples to invite others into the kingdom of God, he reminded them, 'Freely you have received; freely give' (Matt. 10:8). Just as I and my team encourage the Fulbe followers of Jesus to freely give away to others what they have discovered in Jesus, we invite you to join us in this great privilege. Let's not keep Jesus to ourselves, let's give him away!

If you have read this book and are not yet a follower of Jesus, then I encourage you to find someone who can explain to you what this is all about, maybe the person who gave you this book. You too are invited to meet Jesus; he is waiting for you to respond. It will be the best decision you ever make in your life. Remember the stories of Bakka, Adda, Samira, Yaya, Abdou, Mairamou, Jamilla, Mamadou and Saali? Jesus changed the direction of their lives, because what he offers is real and life-giving. Jesus does not invite us to a 'religion', as that consists only of rituals and burdens; instead, Jesus invites us to himself and in so doing he carries our burdens and renews us on the inside. This is his promise: 'Come to me, all who are weary and burdened, and I will give you rest' (Matt. 11:28). The people you have read about in this book ran to Jesus because their hearts were longing for this rest. They believed and discovered that having Jesus at the centre of their lives was worth the cost of being despised by their family and friends because what they found was so much more than what the world has to offer. Jesus described himself as 'The way, the truth and the life' (John 14:6) and proved it by going to the cross for each one of us, then beating death once and for all three days later. If you have never searched to find out who Jesus Christ is and what he has done for you, then please don't let another day go by without checking out his invitation to you. Are you willing to do this? Are you ready to respond to Jesus' invitation to join the multitude? I long to be with you on that day when we are presented to Jesus.

> There before me was a great multitude that no one could count, from every nation, tribe, people and language, standing before the throne and before the Lamb . . . And they cried out in a loud voice:

> 'Salvation belongs to our God,
> who sits on the throne,
> and to the Lamb.'

> Revelation 7:9–10

Appendix 1: A Glimpse at the Workers of Meskine Hospital

With a large workforce of over one hundred and thirty employees, Meskine Hospital has become a community in its own right. Being a non-denominational organization, MCWA has had the freedom to employ people from different religious backgrounds and ethnic groups, leading it to become a mixed family in every sense of the word. No one church tradition or tribal group can claim dominance, which is unusual in the history of Christian medical missions.

Another characteristic of the workforce that has become evident over the years is that people have been employed on their ability to do the job, rather than just the fact that they possess a certificate of training. As is common in many private medical institutions in Cameroon, many of the staff at Meskine Hospital have received 'in-house' teaching and only afterwards have they gone on to receive official, state-recognized training, if it is available. The story of many of Meskine Hospital's leaders and heads of department is truly remarkable when seeing their humble beginnings. Several of them were not able to finish their secondary schooling due to financial struggles. Education is not state-sponsored in Cameroon, so each student's training has to be personally funded each year. Consequently, if you find yourself growing up in a large family of twenty children, there will probably not be enough money for schooling to be a high priority. Many of the employees only managed to get as far as they did in school because they themselves funded it with whatever work they could find, while trying to keep up with their studies. Sheer determination was ingrained in them from an early age. It is not surprising today that many Cameroonian young men and women in their early and mid-twenties are still struggling to finish secondary school, some just running out of steam and resources to get through the last couple of years.

Some of our most capable and esteemed employees came from such a background. Starting out as house helps, cooks and labourers in the early days of Meskine Hospital, their strength of character and intelligence became clear over the years. They were given the opportunity to move into medical work, progressing up the ranks as they responded to the training and mentoring offered them. It has been truly wonderful to see so many excel as they were launched from their humble beginnings to positions of authority and leadership with integrity.

A special day in the calendar of Meskine Hospital is 1 May, the Labour Day holiday in Cameroon. This is the day when all over the country there are parades of workers from all walks of life, celebrating their identity as employees of whatever enterprise they belong to. Meskine Hospital celebrates this day in style. With every employee wearing matching outfits made from the same material, especially printed for the occasion, they proudly take their place in the marching procession in the provincial town, in front of politicians, leaders and members of the public. It has become expected to hear loud cheers and applause from the hundreds of people gathered as the Meskine Hospital employees march along, the wider community expressing their appreciation for all that they do in taking care of the sick. This is a fitting tribute to the employees who are the face and hands of all the care that is given in that place. They are the ones who daily give of themselves to serve those in need coming to them; without them this institution would be nothing more than a shell of lifeless buildings.

Appendix 2: From Baton Rouge to Meskine: the Story of Medical Centers of West Africa

Part 1

It could be said that Baton Rouge, Louisiana, is not the most famous place in the USA to outsiders but it has become well known to a select group of people who live in northern Cameroon. Baton Rouge has been the home of the Medical Centers of West Africa (MCWA) headquarters for the twenty-five years of Meskine Hospital's existence, and several years before that as it was coming into being. Baton Rouge is the connecting point for the three founding families and so holds a special place in the hearts of the hospital family community.

Several journeys, one destination

After Bert and Debbie Oubre were married and returned from working at Mbingo Baptist Hospital in Cameroon in mid-1987, they set up home in Baton Rouge. Having seen the treatment and care that the sufferers of Hansen's disease (also known as leprosy) received at Mbingo, Bert and Debbie moved to Baton Rouge so that Bert could learn more surgical procedures to help with tendon repairs and transplants for these patients. Carville, Louisiana, just outside Baton Rouge, was home to the National Hansen's Disease Centre, so it was the obvious choice for the Oubres to come and live nearby for a time.

The Oubres had seen the effectiveness and huge benefits that a well-run medical facility could achieve at Mbingo, and when they learned of the need in the far north of Cameroon, where Fulbe lived in large numbers, the seed and vision for MCWA became well established. Being a man of action, with plenty of determination to see a plan come into being, Bert's mind went into overdrive as he started to plan what could be done to get MCWA up and running. At the same time, a friend introduced them to The Chapel, which soon became their regular place of worship in Baton Rouge, thus establishing the next steps in the birth of MCWA.

Meanwhile, Scott and Lee Pyles were a newly married couple pursuing their careers in Baton Rouge. Although they were very active members at The Chapel, the pursuit of a comfortable family life was the motivation for their lives at that time. As they were awaiting the arrival of their first child, however, Scott read the biography of Dawson Trotman, which abruptly spoke to his heart and the need to go deeper in his walk with Christ. This began a journey of their eyes being opened to God's heart for the nations; Jesus was still in the business of seeking and saving the lost beyond Baton Rouge. By the end of 1987 Scott and Lee had made a commitment together to be available for God to use to enable other people to hear about Jesus, even if this meant going to a different part of the world. The Chapel became the meeting place of the Oubres and the Pyles; God was clearly bringing his servants together.

The Chapel in Baton Rouge was established in 1972 from the fruit of a Billy Graham visit to the city. Out of the ten thousand people who had turned to Christ from that event, one thousand of them were students from Louisiana State University (LSU). Donald Tabb, then a staff member of the Billy Graham Evangelistic Association, responded to God's call and the invitation of others in Baton Rouge to start a church to meet the spiritual needs of the students and the wider area. It developed into a flourishing Christian community dedicated to making Jesus known and discipling people to walk closely with him. Donald remained the much-loved pastor of the church until 2001. By the time the future MCWA team found themselves worshipping there together it already had a well-established interest in overseas mission work. This had led to the Perspectives on the World Christian Movement course being run there regularly and short-term teams going out to Honduras, which some of the future MCWA team had taken part in.

Lyman Osborne, a successful engineer and businessman, was also a member of The Chapel; he already had a busy life, but it was about to get even busier. He had been impacted by the Perspectives course and was already involved in the mission activities of the church, so after Bert Oubre approached Pastor Donald Tabb and the elders in 1988 about starting a medical project in Cameroon, Lyman was invited along to hear more about it. He had no idea that Cameroon was about to become a big part of his life.

A few months of discussing, praying and developing the idea of the project culminated in an informal gathering in September 1988, where Bert and Debbie were able to share more of their vision to start a medical work in Cameroon, with the purpose of bringing the gospel to the unreached Fulbe people. A group of around fifteen interested people, mostly from The Chapel, gathered to hear what they had to say, including Scott and Lee Pyles, Donald Tabb and Lyman Osborne. The proposal was well received, with a real sense that God was in this plan, so The Chapel felt able to support the Oubres as they went about setting up the organization of MCWA. At this meeting the first directors were appointed and things began to move rather quickly from that moment on.

At that point, 'Africa' and 'Muslims' had not featured on Scott's radar, but he and Lee had been waiting for guidance from God as to where he would have them go for a short-term mission experience. Scott was experiencing frustration as he hadn't received any clear guidance from God yet. As he was praying late one night, he felt God speaking to him very clearly: 'I'm not asking for six months of your time. I'm asking for your whole life. I want you to get involved with what your church is doing. I want you to sell your house and go to seminary and then I want you to join Bert and Debbie Oubre in going to Cameroon.' All of a sudden Scott's thoughts became crystal-clear and a huge wave of peace came over him. He had never experienced God speaking to him so clearly but here it was – God was changing the direction of Scott and Lee's lives forever. At that time Lee was expecting their second child; she was not anticipating hearing that she would be raising her family in Cameroon though. Shock and fear began to take hold, but after a time of praying for God to confirm the way ahead, Lee too experienced an inner peace that this was indeed what God was asking them to do. It took a little longer for their parents and siblings to come around to the idea though. Scott's grandmother summed up their thoughts: 'All our lives we pray for our children, from the time that they are born and as they grow up, that they would honour the Lord and walk with Jesus, and then the minute they tell us that they are going to be missionaries we react in unbelief that God would be leading them that way!'

On 5 January 1989 the Medical Centers of West Africa Inc. (MCWA) was established as a non-profit organization in Louisiana, with Bert Oubre named as the first president of the board of directors. Lyman took over this position later that year and remained so for the next eleven years. His wife Marge was a huge support as MCWA secretary and together they gave of themselves to keep the MCWA HQ functioning, initially out of their home and then into office space donated by The Chapel. The work of getting a team together to go to Cameroon now had a platform to work from, and The Chapel was fully behind them.

Danny and Frances Kennison were also members of the same church as the Oubres and the Pyles, but the couples did not know each other until talk of MCWA began to emerge. The Kennisons' journey to Meskine had begun many years before when they both came to faith in Jesus as students at LSU. They both grew up in church-going families but the concept of knowing Jesus personally had escaped them. When Billy Graham came to Baton Rouge in 1970, Frances discovered a different life with Jesus from spending time with Christian friends, and was ready to commit her life to him, too. Danny attended the same Billy Graham meetings but was not convinced that he needed to change his life until Christian friends invited him to attend a Bible study, which finally opened his eyes to his absolute need of Jesus. Danny and Frances found themselves together in the LSU band, where their friendship began, leading to marriage in 1977. They both entered the teaching profession, but Danny later chose to pursue a career in carpentry and house-building and set up his own successful business. As their little family became established, they did not foresee what was coming next with the birth of their second son, Brady. He was born with multiple disabilities which had not been perceived on pre-birth scans, so the shock to the parents was profound. His short life of eight months was mostly spent in hospital, as he had to undergo seven different surgeries. By this time Danny and Frances were members of The Chapel and the support of this community carried them through those difficult months. For Danny and Frances, it was a time of incredible deepening of their dependence on God as they would see that Brady's short life had blessed them, teaching them invaluable life lessons.

In the spring of 1989 another life-changing event happened to them during a missions conference at The Chapel. For three days they were enthralled by Don Richardson's teaching; for the first time in their lives, Danny and Frances understood from the Bible that God was a missionary God. They heard God calling them to be involved, but they had no idea where it would lead.

Not long after this, an elder from The Chapel asked Danny if he was still in the building business. Danny replied 'yes', hoping that this meant he was being considered for a building project that the church was undertaking. However, the elder's next question proved life-altering for the Kennisons, as he asked, 'Danny, would you like to build a hospital in Cameroon?' to which Danny replied 'Where's Cameroon?!' That simple question was the event that brought the path that they were already on – to go to an unreached people group somewhere in the world – to intersect with the work of MCWA. Within a few months, their lives had completely changed direction from a settled family life in Baton Rouge to uprooting and heading off to Africa.

Bert began to research who else might be interested or have experience of working in northern Cameroon, which led him, Scott and Lyman to visit the office of the Sudan Interior Mission in March 1989. SIM had worked widely across western Africa and the sub-Saharan region for decades but were not working in Cameroon. What SIM were able to help with, though, were the results of a recent survey they had done of the area. It confirmed that the over half a million Fulbe people were indeed mostly unengaged and unreached with the gospel, despite there being several church denominations well established in the area. They also discovered from this survey that there were already a few missionaries who were intentional in getting the gospel out to Fulbe and other Muslims in the northern region of Cameroon. These were encouraging findings for the visitors from MCWA and indicated that they were on the right track; there was definitely a need for their intended work.

In an era before internet and mobile phones, it was determined that the best thing to do was simply travel to the northern region of Cameroon and do their own survey. In June 1989 Bert, Scott and Lyman took the plunge and headed off to Maroua, the provincial capital of the far northern province of Cameroon. Without any French language between them, and as it was Scott's and Lyman's first visit to Africa, it was a memorable, chaotic trip. They had discovered that Swiss and German missionaries from the Sudan United Mission had set up several health clinics in the region and had also established the Union of Evangelical Churches of Cameroon. They wanted to discuss MCWA's plans to see if SUM could help in any way.

Having no contact phone number for SUM, Bert, Scott and Lyman asked around in the town of Maroua until they finally found the SUM compound on the eastern side of town. Here were these three Americans with no German or French language ability, arriving out of the blue asking to speak to the director. However, Kurt Märki and his wife, Elsbeth, were not unaccustomed to unannounced visitors and made their surprise guests very welcome for the next few days. As Bert and the others began to share their vision of the medical work and their desire to reach the Fulbe Muslims with the gospel, Kurt's reaction was initially unenthusiastic. He was rather sceptical that the Fulbe would be receptive, announcing, 'During the thirty years I have been in Maroua, I have only heard of two Fulbe coming to Christ around here – one was killed and the other returned to Islam.' As they continued to talk, though, Kurt recognized the call of God on the MCWA team's lives and did all he could to help them. He took them to see some of SUM's health centres, which helped Scott and Lyman to visualize how different medical care in Africa is compared to the USA.

From their discussions together it seemed that the town of Bogo, a well-known area for Fulbe, might be a good place to investigate regarding where to locate the MCWA project. The four of them went on a trip to the town and were warmly welcomed by the *lamiido* (town chief), who was delighted that they would consider building a new health facility for his people. He assured them that he would gladly give MCWA a large parcel of land for them to build their hospital.

By the end of their visit, Kurt had warmed up to the vision and encouraged Bert to contact the SUM HQ office in Switzerland to talk over how a partnership might be established between them and MCWA. Incredibly, the meeting was arranged on Bert's way home through Europe and the SUM director set aside time at midnight to see him! This cemented the beginning of a friendship which later developed into an official partnership between MCWA and SUM. A cooperative agreement between the two organizations was agreed on a later visit, MCWA recognizing the risk that SUM were taking in supporting this new, untested project. With this agreement it meant that MCWA could come to Cameroon by the invitation of the evangelical church which would be a great help at an official level in Cameroon. This was a major step and encouraged everyone that they were moving in the right direction.

Another huge confirmation that God was in this plan was that by July 1989 all three houses of the Oubres, Pyles and Kennisons had been sold in Baton Rouge during a depressed real-estate market; and all three got their asking prices! This freed them up to go to seminary, raise financial and prayer supporters and go to French-language school in France and Switzerland, which would occupy their time for the next two years. It also became a time for the three families to get to know each other better as, up to this point, they really had not been more than acquaintances, worshipping in the same church. Each couple had young children, so when they all got together they created quite a crowd.

In the meantime Lyman, Marge and the other members of the MCWA board were on a fast track, learning how to run a non-profit organization stateside. Legal issues, finances, protocols and medical supplies became the thoughts that followed them around like shadows. The learning curve was massive for everyone involved. Lyman's words summarize what the MCWA family was feeling in these foundational years: 'I got to be a part of something greater. I participated in something God was doing and just went with the flow.'

Then in 1991 something rather unexpected happened. Up to this point MCWA had been moving in the direction of building the hospital in the town of Bogo, and had made applications to the Cameroonian Government in this vein. When the papers came back granting permission for the hospital to be built, however, Bogo was not named as the location, but the village of Meskine which was fifty miles away, to the west! Bert, Scott and Lyman had not visited Meskine, although their travels on the survey trip had gone nearby. On further investigation, no one was able to explain why or when this change of location came about, or who was responsible. Was it an administrative error? Was it an intentional act on the part of someone with influence who favoured Meskine? Was it an act of God? The papers said 'Meskine' and that was a final decision from the government. So MCWA would be the builders of Meskine Hospital and not Bogo Hospital.

Part 2
Building and opening

Bert, Debbie, daughter Heidi and newly born Philippe Oubre were the first of the team to arrive in Cameroon after the years of preparation, in early 1992. One of Bert's first jobs was to go and visit the *lamiido* of Bogo to apologize for the change of hospital location, explaining that the decision was not his but was taken out of his hands. Then new discussions began with the *lamiido* of Meskine, who was pleased to know that there would soon be a new medical facility for his people. He donated an area of empty land to the north of the village. It was considered to be worthless farmland but was soon to be transformed into a thriving community that was anything but worthless.

The Oubre family initially lived near the SUM missionaries and were able to glean a lot from them as they adjusted to their new life. This was a time of learning and preparation for all that was to come in getting the MCWA project started, networking and finding out how to function and get things done in a new culture; the help of more experienced missionaries was invaluable. This was also the time to get the official papers with the government organized so that MCWA could function as a non-profit organization in its own right, becoming independent of SUM in the long run. Then came the job of recruitment of prospective MCWA employees, starting with labourers, as everything was about construction at this point.

Scott and Lee, with sons Charlie and Michael, arrived in October 1992, and two weeks later Danny and Frances with their sons, Wes and Tyler. The MCWA team was together again and finally in Cameroon.

Preparations for the construction of the hospital had already begun with brick-making in anticipation of Danny's arrival, and trees were planted on the empty plot of land. The building work got going in December with a team of nine men, supervised by Danny and his assistant, who also worked as the translator for Danny. Danny had hit the ground running when he got to Meskine, so any thoughts of extended time set aside for language- and culture-learning were long forgotten! The initial plan was to build a thirty-bed hospital. The first buildings to go up were the dispensary where outpatients would eventually be assessed, with areas for the laboratory, store room for medical supplies and pharmacy. One by one other buildings were added – the surgical 'Bloc', separate wards for men, women and children, and radiography. There were also houses built for the team, starting with the guest-house and the Oubres' home. The construction team continued to be busy for years to come as the number of patients and visiting team members increased, so that by 1997 they had already completed twenty major building projects on the MCWA property.

The three MCWA families were only together for two months in Cameroon, as the Oubres left for their first home assignment to USA at the end of 1992, but by now their roles for the hospital project had been assigned. The recruitment for nursing students was announced in 1993, attracting many hopeful applicants; the training began with sixty students, forty-four persevering to the end. The teachers of the intensive nine-month course were Bert and Debbie, Lee and a doctor from Cameroon, plus help from some short-term visitors who had started to add to the team by then. When Debbie and Lee took a few weeks' maternity leave in 1994 to have Joel and Jessica respectively, the teaching team was depleted temporarily, but the training continued. The two mothers hardly took a breath and picked up where they had left off, with their babies strapped onto the backs of their baby-sitters. This was an intense time of pouring knowledge into the eager young nursing students.

Scott's role as administrator could not really begin until the hospital had been built and the workforce developed, which gave him plenty of time during that first year to intentionally study Fulfulde and the culture. He made the most of it and, being a quick learner, made excellent progress. Both the Pyles and the Kennison families decided to live in the village neighbourhood of Meskine rather than on the hospital grounds as they wanted to be able to interact more with the community. It made sense for the Oubres to live on the hospital grounds though, as Bert would need to be within easy reach of the patients at all times of the day and night once the hospital was opened. Being in the village, Frances also had opportunity to learn Fulfulde and made inroads into this difficult language, while Danny's Fulfulde studies took place on the construction site – consequently he learned all kinds of vocabulary that nobody else knew!

In May 1994, Samaritan's Purse and World Medical Missions (WMM) supported MCWA by sending cargo containers full of medical supplies, which was a huge help in providing a lot of the essential supplies needed to get the hospital started. MCWA continued to be grateful recipients of several donations for years that followed. Several visiting surgeons and physicians also came to Meskine thanks to WMM's vision of sending out short-term help to mission hospitals around the world.

Incredibly, by March 1995 Meskine Hospital was officially opened, although the team had already started seeing patients prior to this. With the new buildings and a team of newly trained nurses, the official opening was held with great thankfulness to God for all that had been achieved to get MCWA to this point. That first year saw 509 surgical cases, but by 1997 this had doubled, and the number of outpatient clinic visits was already rising to nearly 14,000.

Meanwhile, around the same time in Baton Rouge, Lyman and Marge Osborne were grateful to move the new MCWA headquarters into an office at The Chapel. It was a new beginning for the MCWA family, and one that would continue to see growth in the ministry in every way; more short-termers were recruited to help at the hospital and on the board of directors, and more support for the work was raised. It would not be an overstatement to say that the steady flow of short-term volunteers who came to Meskine over the years was life-giving and energy-boosting to the work in every way. Without them there can be no doubt that Meskine Hospital would not be the excellent place of medical care it is today.

New volunteer recruits were not just coming from the USA, though. Because MCWA was partnering with the Swiss branch of SUM, it led to contact with their UK branch too, then called Action Partners (and later to become Pioneers UK). When MCWA started the search for a radiographer to come to Meskine to set up the X-ray and ultrasound department, they were delighted to get a double portion when in 1994 Andy and Rachel Picton from the UK volunteered to come with their little girl Aimee for two years. It was a challenging assignment, as it took so long to get an adequate electricity supply to the hospital, and for the right cable to arrive in Meskine for the X-ray machine to function; it finally turned up and X-rays and ultrasounds have subsequently become a well-used and essential facility. The Pictons were able to leave the department in the capable hands of technicians they had trained.

As the hospital work developed, a physiotherapy department was started when I arrived in 1998, gaining a purpose-built facility in 2000, and further established by visits from Sally and Rachel (physiotherapists from the UK and Australia respectively). It soon became clear that larger facilities would be necessary for maternity care, so a whole new ward was built in 2000, which created more space for deliveries, inpatients and the mother-and-baby care clinics. Pharmacy and medical supplies had also outgrown their homes, so a new facility was built for this in 2002. The last major addition to the hospital was an extensive administration building that reflected the increased workload that this department had undertaken with a growing workforce. What had started out as a plan to build a modest 30-bed hospital in 1992 had gradually evolved, beyond the expectations of all involved, now stretching to over 130 beds at the busiest times.

MCWA-UK

With MCWA's link to the UK through Action Partners and the Picton family, several other missionaries were added to the team in Meskine, notably Dr John and Lesley Baigent, along with their daughter, Hannah. John had worked for twenty-five years as a GP in the UK, but after taking early retirement he and his wife Lesley offered to come and help in Meskine Hospital for six months in 1997. This turned into an incredible extended service spanning eleven years, during which time Dr John led the medical team after the Oubres left in 2001, and helped the hospital to develop and mature as the workload steadily increased. Lesley also made a huge contribution as she took on the management of the guest-house. Dr John was a big man in every way – in body, in voice, in humour, in enthusiasm, in courage and most of all, in his love for Jesus. John would take and make every opportunity possible to share with his patients the joy he experienced in his Saviour.

Through the Baigents' network of support and friendship with Rachel Picton's parents, David and Linda Molden, MCWA-UK was started under their leadership in 1998 to support Meskine Hospital with getting medical supplies and equipment. MCWA-UK also generously contributed to the 'Poor Fund' that was developed to help patients who could not afford to pay their medical bills. This support from the UK has been a great encouragement to the overall work at Meskine over the years.

MCWA World Day of Prayer

Another significant development was the start of the World Day of Prayer for the work of MCWA, which was the brain-child of John Baigent. On 1 February 1998 the MCWA team planned a special day to gather for worship and prayer, bringing their requests and thanksgiving to God. John's mind turned to the many people who had already served in Cameroon from around the world, who became known as 'the Bintu group' – those who had 'been to' Meskine. By 1998 there had already been over eighty visitors to Meskine from the USA, UK, Switzerland, Germany, France, and Australia. As prayer is the powerhouse for God's work, John wanted to recruit the Bintu group to join the MCWA team for this important day. Consequently, the invitation went out around the world to friends and supporters of Meskine Hospital, asking people to fast and pray for MCWA with their families and in their churches. Since that time, MCWA has set aside a day each year to invite people around the world to join in praying and fasting for the work. We can only thank God for all these prayers that have been offered, and all the answers we have experienced as a result. The MCWA story would surely have been very different if this work of prayer had not been so faithfully carried out over so many years.

Meanwhile, in Baton Rouge

The development of Meskine Hospital into a bustling medical service could only have happened with the incredible support that continued from MCWA HQ in Baton Rouge. Lyman Osborne served in the role of president until February 2001 when he handed over the reins to Dr Leo Yoder, who had already been serving on the board of directors. Although these men fulfilled the same leadership role, it was not the same task, as MCWA had changed so much since the beginning. Lyman had been the perfect man to get things established, with his skills in organization, business experience and methodical way of working, along with his humility and willingness to learn as he went along. All this ensured that the work was in safe hands right from the outset. With Marge working alongside him so efficiently, the formative years of MCWA had been built on a steady foundation. The field team recognized that the HQ team had worked so hard and given as much blood and sweat as they had done in Meskine, even if the air-conditioning had helped a little in Baton Rouge! By 2001 the hospital was getting to be at its most busy, with the number of beds up to 120 and a growing employee list, so with all his medical experience as a doctor, stateside and overseas, it was perfect timing to have Leo Yoder at HQ. A visit to Meskine in November of 2001 added significantly to Leo's understanding of the context and the work.

That year MCWA hosted a gathering of friends at The Chapel with the purpose of recruiting future board members. As in any organization, there tends to be a turnover of people who are willing and able to serve in this way, so MCWA kept an antenna up to find people who had the vision, time and desire to join the board. Over the years several of them have visited Meskine Hospital, which has always been an encouragement to the field team and the hospital employees; for the board members themselves it has proven to ignite their passion and understanding of MCWA even more. Nothing beats a personal visit to Meskine to understand how the hospital functions.

One of these visitors to Meskine was Bill Bordelon, and so it was fitting that he was named president of MCWA in 2005 for the following two years. He then handed over to Kenny Dunaway, who also visited the field to see the work for himself. His role changed in 2012 to become chairman of the board, while a new leadership position was created for Cheryl Yennie, who was named executive director. This reflected the changing leadership that was required, as there was now too much work at the MCWA HQ to be carried out by volunteers alone.

Cheryl gave up her career as a successful accountant, becoming full-time support for the field team. When Cheryl was invited to join the MCWA board of directors in 2002, she had no idea that it was about to change her life. In her own words, reflecting on the impact of joining MCWA staff, she remarks, 'I was forever changed and my life was no longer ordinary!' Since leading the HQ team, Cheryl has made several visits to Cameroon and has been an incredible support to the field team with her wise counsel, and her accounting skills, keeping the hospital going in the right direction. Under her leadership there have been extreme challenges for the work in the field, but she has been one of the anchors that have steadied MCWA through the changes and the storms. At the time of writing, Cheryl is supported in her role by Matt Heinz, who became the chairman of the board in February 2016.

After 25 years, Meskine Hospital now annually serves over 35,000 outpatients, nearly 5,000 inpatients, carries out 1,500 surgical procedures, delivers 300 babies, treats 2,200 physio-therapy patients, takes 8,500 X-rays, does over 86,000 lab tests, builds 100 walking aids, manages 175 people with TB, and employs 130 people. This is what God has done in moving willing people from Baton Rouge to Meskine. To God be all the glory.

Contact Information

For further information about the organizations that have been part of Meskine Hospital's story, please contact:

MCWA at www.mcwestafrica.com
Pioneers UK at www.pioneers-uk.org
Kerry can be contacted at bloodsweatandjesus@gmail.com

Bibliography

Ali, Abdullah Yusuf. *The Holy Qur'an: Translation and Commentary* (Birmingham: Islamic Propagation Centre International, 1946).

Aljazeera Media Network. 'Death Toll in Boko Haram Attack on Nigerian Base Rises to 48', 3, 20 September 2018 (copyright 2020) https://www.aljazeera.com/news/2018/09/death-toll-boko-haram-attack-nigerian-base-rises-48-180903152458851.html (accessed 1 May 2020).

BBC News. 'Who are Nigeria's Boko Haram Islamist Group?' 24 November 2016 (copyright 2020 BBC) https://www.bbc.co.uk/news/world-africa-13809501 (accessed 1 May 2020).

Campbell, John and Asch Harwood, for Council on Foreign Relations. 'Boko Haram's Deadly Impact' 20 August 2018 (copyright 2020) https://www.cfr.org/article/boko-harams-deadly-impact (accessed 1 May 2020).

Ford, Sarah. *Raindrops on a Tin Roof* (self-published, 2017).

Garrison, David. *A Wind in the House of Islam* (Monument, CO: WIGTake Resources, 2014).

Institute for Health Metrics and Evaluation, Seattle, USA. 'Cameroon: What Causes the Most Deaths?' (2017) http://www.healthdata.org/cameroon (accessed 1 May 2020).

Global Recordings Network, https://globalrecordings.net/en/resources (accessed May 2020).

Joshua Project (2020), https://joshuaproject.net (accessed May 2020).

Livingstone, Greg. *Planting Churches in Muslim Cities: A Team Approach* (Grand Rapids, MI: Baker Academic, 1993).

Qureshi, Nabeel. *No God but One: Allah or Jesus?* (Grand Rapids, MI: Zondervan, 2016).

Qureshi, Nabeel. *Seeking Allah, Finding Jesus* (Grand Rapids. MI: Zondervan, 2014).

Regis, Helen A. *Fulbe Voices: Marriage, Islam and Medicine in Northern Cameroon* (Boulder, CO: Westview Press, 2002).

Sahih al-Bukhari, Volume 9, Book 83, number 17, https://www.sahih-bukhari.com/Pages/Bukhari_9_83.php (accessed 1 May 2020).

Serhan, Yasmeen. 'Is ISIS More Violent during Ramadan?' *The Atlantic* (26 June 2017) https://www.theatlantic.com/international/archive/2017/06/is-isis-more-violent-during-ramadan/531444 (accessed 1 May 2020).

United Nations High Commissioner for Refugees (UNHCR). 'Nigeria Situation, UNHCR Regional Update Number 21, 1–29 February 2016' https://www.refworld.org/pdfid/56fcd1b64.pdf (accessed 1 May 2020).

United Nations press release, 20 May 1998, New York (copyright 2014), https://www.un.org/press/en/1998/19980520.eco5759.html (accessed 1 May 2020).

World Population Review. 'Cameroon Population 2020' (2020) http://worldpopulationreview.com/countries/cameroon-population (accessed 1 May 2020).

Notes

1 What Happens When Terrorists Move In

[1] BBC News, 'Who are Nigeria's Boko Haram Islamist Group?' 24 November 2016 (copyright 2020 BBC) https://www.bbc .co.uk/news/world-africa-13809501 (accessed 1 May 2020): Boko Haram was founded in Nigeria in 2002, the initial vision being to oppose Western education and promote Islamic teachings. The group's official name, 'Jama'atu Ahlis Sunna Lidda'awati wal-Jihad' in Arabic, means 'People Committed to the Propagation of the Prophet's Teachings and Jihad'. Locally, however, it was called 'Boko Haram' which, in the Hausa language of the region, generally means 'Western education is forbidden'. Boko Haram launched military operations in 2009 in an attempt to overthrow the Nigerian Government and form an Islamic state, under the increasingly ruthless leadership of Aboubakar Shekau. Attack targets were primarily police stations and other government buildings, later progressing to bombing churches, bus ranks, bars, military barracks, even the police and UN headquarters in the capital, Abuja. These activities were mirrored by a growing wave of Islamist groups further afield in Mali and Somalia, and Islamic State in Syria and Iraq. Shekau pledged allegiance to Islamic State in August 2014, declaring he had established an Islamic caliphate in the region of Gwozo town in Borno State, Nigeria.

2   An 'unreached people group' is a people group with such low numbers of Jesus-followers and resources that outside assistance is needed to reach the rest of their people with the gospel. In May 2020, the Joshua Project (https://joshuaproject.net) reported that 42.5 per cent of the global population are still classed as being unreached with the gospel.

3   United Nations High Commissioner for Refugees, 'Nigeria Situation, UNHCR Regional Update Number 21, 1–29 February 2016' https://www.refworld.org/pdfid/56fcd1b64.pdf (accessed 1 May 2020) reported that there were over 60,000 refugees scattered around Cameroon and over 160,000 internally displaced people. Compared to the 2.2 million internally displaced people in Nigeria, however, this was only a fraction of the people who had been forced to abandon their homes due to terrorist activity.

4   Aljazeera Media Network, 'Death toll in Boko Haram Attack on Nigerian Base Rises to 48', 3 September 2018 (copyright 2020) https://www.aljazeera.com/news/2018/09/death-toll-boko-haram-attack-nigerian-base-rises-48-180903152458851.html (accessed 1 May 2020). However, on 20 August 2018, John Campbell and Asch Harwood, Council on Foreign Relations, 'Boko Haram's Deadly Impact' (copyright 2020) https://www.cfr.org/article/boko-harams-deadly-impact (accessed 1 May 2020) reported that the number was even higher at over 30,000.

5   This team had been expertly coached and mentored by Scott Pyles, and by Danny Kennison and John Baigent for a time. See Appendix 1 for a glimpse of the Meskine Hospital employees.

6   This is a system to allocate degrees of urgency to wounds or illnesses, deciding the order of treatment of a large number of patients so that the most urgent are dealt with as soon as possible.

2 From the Deep South to the Far North

1   For the full story of the development of MCWA and Meskine Hospital, see Appendix 2.

2 The story of the Tower of Babel is found in Gen. 11:1–9, where God caused confusion among the people of the earth so that they became divided into different language groups.

3 People from Many Tribes and Nations

1 Helen A. Regis, *Fulbe Voices: Marriage, Islam and Medicine in Northern Cameroon* (Boulder, CO: Westview Press, 2002) gives an interesting explanation and insight into the Fulbe life and culture.

2 Muslim men who have taken the pilgrimage to Mecca.

4 Seeing the Hospital for the First Time

1 World Population Review, 'Cameroon Population 2020' (2020) https://worldpopulationreview.com/countries/cameroon-population (accessed 1 May 2020).

2 This story of Nicodemus coming to Jesus can be found in John 3:1–15.

5 The Prayer Round

1 *Baaba* is the Fulfulde word for 'father'.

2 The Bible talks about being 'clothed with Christ' in Gal. 3:27.

6 When Only an Operation Will Do

1 World Wide Fund for Nature/World Wildlife Fund.

2 Dr John Baigent worked for many years as a GP in the UK. After he took early retirement he and his wife, Lesley, and daughter, Hannah, offered to come and help in Meskine Hospital for

six months in 1997, while Dr Oubre took a much-needed furlough. This turned into service spanning eleven years, during which time Dr John led the medical team after the Oubres left in 2001.

[3] David and Patsy Alfors, from the USA, joined our team as long-termers in Meskine in 2004. They were seconded to MCWA from ReachGlobal, the missionary branch of the Evangelical Free Church of America.

[4] Local chief, or king, in the Fulfulde language.

[5] Dr Jacqueline Koster, from the Netherlands, served in Meskine for fifteen years from 1998 onwards, in community health education, general practice and outreach to Muslims with the gospel. She had previously served for ten years in Nigeria.

7 Can Anyone Else Help Us?

[1] https://www.willingandabel.org.uk (accessed 1 May 2020).

[2] Sarah Ford, a physician's assistant from the USA, served in Meskine for two years from 2008 to 2010. For more of her experiences in Meskine, and Aissa's full story, see Sarah Ford's self-published book, *Raindrops on a Tin Roof* (2017). This extract under the heading 'Aissa' is an edited version of original, published here with Sarah Ford's agreement.

8 An Epidemic Hidden in Shame

[1] United Nations press release (20 May 1998) https://www.un.org/press/en/1998/19980520.eco5759.html, regarding poverty eradication (accessed 1 May 2020).

[2] The Old Testament prophet Isaiah prophesied that the Messiah 'took up our pain and bore our suffering' in Isa. 53:4. In Matt. 8:17 we learn that Jesus is the fulfilment of this as he 'took up our infirmities and bore our diseases'.

3   Jesus talks about being 'born again' in John 3:3–8, referring to the new spiritual life we gain when we believe in him.

9 Learning to Walk Again

1   Institute for Health Metrics and Evaluation, Seattle, USA, 'Cameroon: What Causes the Most Deaths?' (2017) http://www. healthdata.org/cameroon (accessed 1May 2020). As recorded for 2017, road traffic accidents were the ninth highest cause of death in Cameroon.
2   These stories can be found in John 5:2–9 and Acts 3:1–10.

10 Baby Jesus in the Bush

1   Jesus describes himself as the Good Shepherd in John 10:11–18.
2   Those who become believers and followers of Jesus Christ are described as being 'new creations' in 2 Cor. 5:17.
3   '*Baaba* and *Daada* Aisatou' means 'Father and Mother of Aisatou'. The common Fulbe way to address people is according to their family status such as 'Father of . . .' or 'Mother of . . .', rather than by proper names. Scott and Lee's daughter, Jessica, was born in Meskine and the village named her Aisatou, so from then on Scott and Lee were known as *Baaba* and *Daada* Aisatou.

11 Faith, Fear and Fruitfulness

1   Greg Livingstone's book, *Planting Churches in Muslim Cities: A Team Approach* (Grand Rapids, MI: Baker Academic, 1993) became a starting point for our team.
2   Nabeel Qureshi's books excellently explain these differences between the Muslim and Christian faiths and views of Jesus. I highly recommend reading his books: *Seeking Allah, Finding Jesus* (Grand Rapids, MI: Zondervan, 2014) and *No God but One: Allah or Jesus?* (Grand Rapids, MI: Zondervan, 2016).

3   https://globalrecordings.net/en/resources.

4   Jesus taught his disciples to be influencers of society, likening it to being 'salt and light', as recorded in Matt. 5:13–16.

5   There are many books written about DMMs, but the main thrust of the strategy comes from Jesus' teaching in the gospels (Matt. 10 and Luke 9:1–6; 10:1–20).

6   These mentions of the work of the Holy Spirit in our lives can be found in John 14:15–17; 16:7–15.

7   This means that there are disciples of Jesus who have led some others to Christ, who then led some to Christ, who then led some to Christ, who then led some to Christ. An example of this is Paul's words in 2 Tim. 2:2.

8   *A Wind in the House of Islam* by David Garrison (Monument, CO: WIGTake Resources, 2014) gives an excellent account of this.

12 Singing Her Own Song

1   'Anyone who after accepting faith in Allah utters unbelief except under compulsion his heart remaining firm in faith but such as open their breast to unbelief on them is wrath from Allah and theirs will be a dreadful penalty.' Abdullah Yusuf Ali, *The Holy Qur'an: Translation and Commentary* (Birmingham: Islamic Propagation Centre International, 1946), Qur'an 16:106.

2   *Sahih al-Bukhari*, Volume 9, Book 83, number 17 states: 'Allah's Apostle said, "The blood of a Muslim who confesses that none has the right to be worshipped but Allah and that I am His Apostle, cannot be shed except in three cases: In Qisas for murder, a married person who commits illegal sexual intercourse and the one who reverts from Islam (apostate) and leaves the Muslims."' https://www.sahih-bukhari.com/Pages/Bukhari_9_83.php (accessed 1 May 2020).

13 The Hardest Month of the Year

[1] Yasmeen Serhan, 'Is ISIS More Violent during Ramadan?' The Atlantic (26 June 2017) https://www.theatlantic.com/international/archive/2017/06/is-isis-more-violent-during-ramadan/531444/ (accessed 1 May 2020).

[2] Ephesians 2:8–9 emphasizes this gift of salvation that God offers us in Jesus Christ, thus rendering our good works redundant in an effort to save ourselves. Jesus has already done the work for us.

Authentic

We trust you enjoyed reading this book
from Authentic. If you want to be
informed of any new titles from this author
and other releases you can sign up to the
Authentic newsletter by scanning below:

Online:
authenticmedia.co.uk

Follow us: